ML00038969

GENDER EQUALITY
IN
ISLAM

By

Dr. Farid Younos

© 2002 by Dr. Farid Younos. All rights reserved.

No part of this book may be reproduced, stored in a retrieval system, or transmitted by any means, electronic, mechanical, photocopying, recording, or otherwise, without written permission from the author.

ISBN: 1-4033-5703-X (e-book)
ISBN: 1-4033-5704-8 (Paperback)

Library of Congress Control Number: 2002093516

This book is printed on acid free paper.

Printed in the United States of America
Bloomington, IN

1stBooks – rev. 10/11/02

IN THE NAME OF ALLAH, MOST GRACIOUS, MOST MERCIFUL

TO MY WIFE, FOWZIA

CONTENTS

ACKNOWLEDGEMENTS

My research would not have been accomplished without the support of many Afghan men and women in the United States. This work is the result of my study of Islam while I have lived in the United States. For the last nine years I have had a TV talk show for the Afghan community in Fremont, California and for five years in Vancouver, Canada. The Afghan people who saw the shows, which aired topics concerning the equality between men and women, encouraged me to write this book. I'm strongly indebted for the valuable recommendations of my dearest friend, Professor Hanif Sherali of Virginia Tech, who read the manuscript. Certainly, I would not have been able to finish this work without the technical support and computer know how of Azeem Sherali, a pre-med student at Johns Hopkins University. Azeem not only helped as a technical assistant, but as a young American Muslim he also questioned some themes or treatises that I brought into this research. He provided in-depth reasoning as to how contemporary Muslims should face and solve their problems within the realm of Western culture while living as good Muslims. Also, I am very grateful to my dear friend Eleanor Smith Montgomery for editing the manuscript. Not only that, but Ellie has also been a wonderful support throughout these years for which I am very blessed. I am grateful for the financial contributions of those individuals and associations listed below. Their monetary support made it possible for me to have my research published.

Afghan Elderly Association, Afghan Women Association International, Dr. Dawn Marie Wadle, Mr. Hussain Nusratty, Mr. Sayed Na'im, Haji Abdul Qudus Faiez, Ms. Nahid Noor, Rev. Richard Mitchell, Ms. Nabila Ahrari and family, Ms. Carolyn Krantz, Mr. Ahmad Zia Karimi and Mrs. Nahid Karimi, Dr. Naser Keshawarz and Mrs. Jamila Keshawarz, Dr.Wahid Momand and Mrs. Nazema Momand, Mr. Basir Momand and Mrs. Diana Payenda Momand, Dr. Fazel Ahmad Abdiani, Mr. Ghulam Sakhi Taymuree and Mrs. Hafifa Taymuree, Mr. Abdul Wadood Zafari, Mr. Hamed Sulaiman and Mrs. Shaima sulaiman, Ms. Liza Muzaffery, Dr. Akhtar Mostamandy and Mrs. Salma Mostamandy, Haji Abdul Hadi Karimzada and Mrs. Najia Karimzada, Mr. Sayed Qadir Hashimi, Mr. Na'im Mojaddidi, Mr. Amir Mohammad kaify and Mrs. Fatima Kaify, Mr. Rahim Shansab and Mrs. Malalai Shansab, Mr. Wais Hakimi and Mrs. Nasrin Hakimi, Mr. Faiz Mohammad Nodrat and Mrs. Zobaida Nodrat, Mr. Abdullah Qassemi and Mrs. Salma Qassemi, Mr Sayed Mir Mohammad Assef Hussaini, Mr. Waissudin Qassemi and Mrs. Mariam Qassemi, Mr. Majid Moalikyar and Mrs. Danesh Moalikyar, Mrs. Karima Qassemi, Mrs. Farzana Moalikyar, and Mr. Hamidullah Mohsini, Dr. Sayed Abdullah Kazem and Mrs. Razia Kazem, Ms. Karima Abhat, Mr. Khair Mohammad Moaliji and Mrs. Gulmakai Moaliji, Mr. Khoja Homayoun Siddiqi and Mrs. Homaira Siddiqi, Mr. Basir Kabir and Mrs. Zakia Kabir, Mr. Hedayatullah Mohammadi and Mrs. Nasrin Mohammadi, Mr. Anwar Necko and Mrs. Nooria Necko, Dr. Sarwar Nassery and Mrs. Najiba Nassery, Mr. Mohammad Samai Sulaiman and Mrs. Nassima

Sulaiman, Mr. Kabir Aziz and Mrs. Nahid Aziz, Mr. Khoja Sarwar Siddiqi and Mrs. Maimuna Siddiqi, Mr. Aresh Omar and Mrs. Shakila Imami Omar, Mr. Mustafa Ismail and Mrs. Zohra Murtaza. Finally, I am thankful to my wife Fowzia both her enormous support and also for her encouragement that I finish my research.

PREFACE

With the emergence of the Taliban forces in Afghanistan in September of 1996, and because of the atrocities they committed against women in that war-stricken country, I was urged to conduct research on the status of women in the Islamic faith. Even though the Taliban are now gone, their beliefs are not, and this topic is still in dire need of discussion and thought.

Many have written on the issue of women in Islam, trying to show that men and women are equal in Islam. These writers, however, always end up alluding to the false idea that not only should women be submissive to men, but also that their roles in the family and in society are unequal to those of men. Consequently, Islamic societies are perceived to be male-dominated environments where women do not have any role in the infrastructure of the social system. In other words, without much Qura'nic or *Sunnah* (traditions of the Prophet) justification, these writers have demonstrated a woman's dependency on the men in her family. Additionally, these writers note the inequality of women participating in the social system and attribute this inequality has been dictated by Islam because of the emotional nature of women.

To show the fairness and superiority of Islam, almost all writers have compared the Islamic faith to pre-Islamic civilizations, i.e. Rome, Greece, India. We need, however, to assess the status of women in the contemporary world. Looking at Islamic and other cultures, we need to compare the roles of women in today's family, as well as in the social and political systems. This is not to say that women in non-Muslim societies are better off; indeed, women in the West are abused, but there *are* women in the Western societies who hold positions of prime importance. Unfortunately, in Islamic societies, women are deprived of their social responsibilities. The time has come to leave the pre-Islamic comparison aside and to find out in the light of Islamic research and social reasoning if men and women are really equal. And if they are equal, then why do men control women's social positions, and make decisions for them?

The first objective of this research project is to show that men and women are equal in all aspects of life in Islam. To accomplish this goal, this research studies men and women in three aspects of life: men and women in creation, men and women in society, and lastly, men and women in the family.

It is important to note that only those *Ahaadith* (traditions and sayings) of the Prophet have been selected that directly correspond to the Qur'an. This is vital for Islamic studies because after the death of the Prophet, many fake *Ahaadith* have appeared, some of which are beyond the logic of Islam in character and out of keeping with the personality of the Prophet. Recognized as the most prominent scholar of *Hadith*, Imam Bukhari had selected 7,275 *hadith* (sayings and traditions of the Prophet) out of 300,000. From these 7,275 *Ahaadith* almost 3000 are repetitious. Imam Abu Hanifa has endorsed only sixteen! [1] If this is true about Imam Abu Hanifa, a prominent Muslim scholar,

---

[1] Hassan, Ibrahim Hassan. The political history of Islam. Trans into Persian Abul Qassem Payenda 1376 of hijra, P.284

and if the Egyptian historian Dr. Hassan's research is valid, we need to be very careful about the selection of the *hadith*. This is not to say the other *Ahaadith* are invalid; rather, it means we should rely on those *Ahaadith* that not only relate to the Qur'an but also relate to the character of the Prophet as well as his mission to humanity.

To do research without bias, a researcher has to live in a free society, where there is freedom to think and freedom from fear and pressure. The United States provides an opportunity for the investigator to conduct research without fearing prosecution or the imprisonment of the mind by narrow-minded individuals or autocratic governments. The time has come that we should export Islamic ideas from America to the rest of the world.

Dr. Farid Younos
Bay Point, California

INTRODUCTION

Unfortunately, all over the world there are injustices against women. Ironically, a few individuals have used the name of Islam to deprive Muslim women of the rights given to them by Islam! Women in these Islamic countries do not have much access to the original sources of Islam and thus believe that what is dictated to them is the word of God or the Prophet. In this way, women have come to be considered possessions of men, and men make all decisions for women. For instance, women cannot work without a man's permission, and in some Islamic countries women are not permitted to drive, and in another women are not permitted to ride a bicycle! Because of the Islamic law, men are the providers and the sole decision-makers. In many families, women have to ask their husbands for permission to visit friends and even their own relatives! If a woman disobeys her husband, she is damned to hell. Also, women are denied the opportunity to govern as some do not think they are as capable as a man. In these countries, women are deprived of social equality, education, and even their right to divorce.

There are a variety of abuses and atrocities that are committed in Islamic societies. I mention a few of them that are of international concern. Crimes of honor,[2] when men brutally kill, burn, or maim their wives and daughters if they suspect that the women

---

[2] Constable, Pamela. "'Honor Killings' Under Attack," *Contra-Costa Times* May 27, 2000.

have had a forbidden relationship or if they have disobeyed them, are committed against women in Islamic countries. Regrettably, the justification for this crime is somehow related to the Islamic faith. The question is, why don't the *ulema* (men of knowledge) take a firm stand against the honor crimes and practice *qisas* (eye for an eye)? Islam is a faith of justice and equality, not a faith of crime, torture, and terrorism. Lamentably, the "men of knowledge" overlook this problem, but they need to know that they will be liable in the hereafter.

In Egypt, where Al-Azhar, the largest Islamic University, is located, people traditionally practice Female Genital Mutilation (FGM). The main reason for this practice is to subdue a woman's sexual enjoyment, which is their natural and Islamic right. In fact, "clinical considerations and the majority of studies in women's enjoyment of sex suggest that genital mutilation does impair a women's enjoyment."[3] As one pro-FGM woman said, "circumcision makes women clean, promotes virginity and chastity and guards young girls from sexual frustration by deadening their sexual appetite."[3] Islam sees human sexuality as part of the natural rights of both males and females and also as important to both genders' psychological and behavioral development. As a matter of fact, early Muslim scholars "believed that sexual deprivation could lead to mental and physical disturbances bordering on insanity. One observer related that a group of people had decided to abstain for ascetic reasons, but soon they developed physical as well as mental abnormalities, especially depression

---

[3] http://www.amnesty.org/ailib/intcam/femgen/fgm1.htm

and fatigue. It was widely believed that sexual deprivation was contrary to the preservation of the human species, harmful to health, and destructive to moral integrity. It was, therefore in the interest of the individual and society that sexual relationships be sanctioned and regulated, not condemned or ignored."[4] Thus, Islam strongly supports the sexual rights of women.

The Taliban did not see the female sector of society as an integral part of the Afghan social system. Using the pretext of national security, the Taliban under the name of Islam banned women from working and from receiving an education. For this reason, "on November 10, 1995, UNICEF issued an official communiqué announcing that it was suspending assistance to education programmes in those parts of Afghanistan where girls were excluded from education."[5] Dr. Garvey from New Jersey City University reported on May 25, 2000, "in 1998 Physicians for Human Rights did a well-publicized study of Afghan women's health, showing grave depression and suicidal tendencies; Amnesty International had declared the entire female population of Afghanistan prisoners of conscience." These problems stemmed from the oppressive Taliban regime that did not have a broad perspective of Islamic civilization and culture. Since the Taliban's understanding of Islam was village-bound, they failed

---

[4] Ati, Hammmudah Abd al. The Family Structure in Islam American Trust Publications, Indiana, 1977.
[5] Dupree, Nancy Hatch. "Afghan Women Under the Taliban," Fundamentalism Reborn? Ed. William Maley, New York, University Press, 1998.

to see the breadth and scope of Islam as a world civilization. A journalist once asked a Talib about *burka,* a head-to-toe covering of women including the face and the eyes. He queried, "If a Talib sees a woman wearing a head scarf but no *burka,* what will happen to her?" The Talib replied, "She will be whipped. If they see a girl and a boy talking together, they will take them to the stadium and lash them."[6]

To see and study gender equality in Islam, three sources are necessary. First is the Qur'an. Second is the tradition of the Prophet. Third is the history of Islam in Madina during the period where the first Islamic social system was established under the direct leadership of the Prophet of Islam, Prophet Mohammad, and later under the first four Caliphs, representatives or heads of state in a Muslim community. After that period, the Islamic system has become biased in regards to social equality between men and women. Also, it is important to note that the first interpreter of the Qur'an was the Prophet of Islam who was under direct guidance from Allah. Later, *ulema* also interpreted and gave their own reasoning; these interpretations are not the work of the Prophet but men of knowledge who did not have the divine revelations.

We first need to answer the question: Does God discriminates in His own creation? If He does discriminate against His creation, then God is not just, and we better not even pursue this study. If He does not discriminate between men and women, then why

---

[6] Vollmann, William T. "Across the Divide: What do the Afghan people think of the Taliban?" The New Yorker, May 15, 2000.

do we allow men to discriminate and pollute God's message as they have done over the centuries?

A second question comes to mind: What is the purpose of His creation? We need to find out whether the definition of worship, which is the purpose of creation, is different between men and women. A third question needs to be asked: Do men and women complement each other as the product of nature? If they do complement each other, then why are women treated as a puppet in the hands of men?

These are the issues that we look at in this manuscript with a clear vision. This vision is the vision of *tawhid*: God is one; the universe is one; mankind is one, and knowledge is one. Therefore, before we discuss the issue of gender, we must study the vision, the purpose of creation, and the responsibility of man as being the representative of God on earth.

TAWHID: THE ISLAMIC WORLDVIEW AND VISION

Tawhid literally translates as Oneness of God. That God is The One and the Only;

"He neither begets nor is He begotten."(Qur'an 112:3).

In a broader sense, God is Absolute; He is the Provider, the Sustainer, the Protector and the Creator. All knowledge comes from Him. He is the lawgiver and the Ruler. God created the universe and mankind for a purpose.

In *tawhid* everything comes from God and all returns to Him. God is the beginning and the end. God is unique in His nature; nothing resembles Him; nothing is like Him. In *tawhid* man is part of nature, and nature is part of man. Man has been created from dust and will become dust again. The main core of *tawhid is God.*[7]

In *tawhid* there is no duality, no discrimination, no superiority and no inferiority. Every creature is created for a purpose and is not created in vain. Every living thing on this earth plays a role for completing the life cycle for others.

Tawhid does not recognize servitude to any other being but God. Therefore, *tawhid* is a liberating force. It liberates mankind from any sort of tyranny and

---

[7] Al faruqi, I. Tawhid: its implications for thought and life. P.1

1

oppression. Even a wife is not entitled to obey her husband if he moves in the opposite direction of *tawhid*. No ruler, no leader, and no head of state should be obeyed in an Islamic state if his attitude and actions are against *tawhid*.

When Islam speaks of man, it is in the gender-neutral form. The statements apply to all men and all women. Just as in the animal and vegetation kingdoms, men and women complement each other under the umbrella of *tawhid*. In other words, *tawhid* allows men and women not only to complement and complete each other but also to grow with each other.

"*[God is the One who] sent water down from the sky and thereby We brought forth pairs of plants each separate from the other.*"(Qur'an 20:53)

"One of a pair is the translation of *zawj* (plural *azwaj*) whose original meaning is that which, in the company of another, forms a pair. The word may just as readily be applied to a married couple as to a pair of shoes."[8] This growth cannot be achieved if they are separated, for the making of life would be incomplete. This is not to say that men and women should be together for the purpose of reproduction only and not in any other engagement. In Islam to achieve a healthy society, both sexes play an equal part in the development of social order. In the time of prayer,

---

[8] Bucaille, Maurice. <u>What is the Origin of Man? The Answers of Science and the Holy Scriptures</u>. Paris, Seghers, 1976, p.168.

women stand behind the men. In *tawaf* (circumambulation) of Ka'bah (house of God built by the Prophet Abraham and his son Ismail in Mecca), men and women circumambulate together. The Qur'an clearly states:

> *"You are the best of people, evolved for mankind, enjoining what is right, forbidding what is wrong." (Qur'an 3:110).*

This verse shows that men and women are jointly responsible to Allah for all that they do.

Worshiping in the Islamic faith means more than praying five times a day. *Ibadah* (worship) comes from *abd* (voluntary servitude or a total obedience to God). Either a person surrenders to the Will of Allah or rejects it. Therefore, whoever obeys God and His Prophet, he/she is in a state of worship. Through worship man will achieve his/her goal, not only for the hereafter but also in this life. If man prays, he/she will purify his/her soul and not let sin or evil thoughts pollute his/her heart, which is the center of God's consciousness. If a Muslim man or woman seeks knowledge, he/she will pave his/her way for excellence in this world as well as in the hereafter. In Islam, life on earth is the bridge for the hereafter. It is through worship that God will bestow His mercy on humanity. As He says in the Qur'an:

> *"And obey Allah and the Messenger, that you may obtain mercy."(Qur'an 3:132).*

Worship, according to Islam, is not only comprised of meditation, thinking about the universe, and concentrating the mind and soul, but it is also accepting the Law of God for complete guidance. As a matter of fact, the Law of God and the law of nature are the same. Thus, when a person surrenders to the Will of God, he/she aligns himself/herself with the natural process of life ordained by God. In other words, when a person acts according to the Qur'an, he/she will be on track without any difficulty, and he/she will have a total peace of mind and soul. God is the lawgiver, and His law is the law of nature given to mankind for peace and tranquility, for civility and modesty, for prosperity and dignity. The problem with today's thinking stems from those people that believe that man is a separate entity and is not part of nature. Thus, they make laws for themselves in order to have civility. Nowadays, humanity's misery stems from mankind's detaching itself from the natural law, God's law.

The creation of Eve was not solely for the reproduction of mankind. Eve was created so that both sexes would complete and complement each other and manage to bring a social order that would be entirely different from that of the animal kingdom. Adam as a social entity would not have reached his completion had not Eve been created. Eve came to this world to mature and complement man, and not to cause the fall of man as the Christian doctrine wrongfully dictates. "The revelation rejects the idea that woman married man to commit the original sin. Thus, Muslim doctrine has never used [such] irreverent terms as did some of the Christian Church fathers who, for a long time, considered woman as 'the agents of the devil.' On the contrary, the Qur'an grants the gift of perfection to two women. Asiyah, the wife of Pharaoh, and Mary, 'daughter of Imran' and mother of Jesus."[9] The Qur'an does not accuse Eve of disobedience or of seduction. Both Adam and Eve were equally responsible for their actions. As stated in the Qur'an:

"In the result, they both ate of the tree, and so their nakedness appeared to them. They began to sew together, for their covering leaves from the Garden: Thus did Adam disobey his Lord, and allow himself to be seduced."(Qur'an 20:21)

In the above verse three issues are clear: First, both were responsible for their actions. Second, "they began to sew together," indicates that both men and women, not just men, are responsible for their dignity and self-consciousness as active social entities. Third, according to this verse, it was Adam who disobeyed and did not find his way out until God Almighty showed him the right path by saying:

"But his Lord chose him (for His Grace): he turned to him, and gave him guidance."(Qur'an 20:122)

In the social context *Tawhid* is the unity of mankind with God. God shows the right path because

---

[9] Boisard, marcel A. Humanism in Islam. American Trust Publication, Indaina, 1988

he knows His own creation and knows what is best for humanity. Without His guidance, mankind is lost. When God says that He is the cherisher and sustainer of the worlds[10], He meant He knows exactly mankind's need, how to lead the universe, and how to educate mankind. The Qur'an says:

> *"He who taught the use of the pen; taught man that which he knew not."(Qur'an 96:4-5).*

Therefore, mankind, being either man or woman, needs Him, not vice-versa; for in keeping with Islam, all creation takes place with God's permission and will. Mankind has a truce or an obligation to God: to fulfill God's mission on Earth. Consistent with Islamic theology, God allowed humans to come to this world to fulfill His mission and to act according to His laws. This truce, made before the advent of the first humans, makes mankind responsible to God in the hereafter for all that has been done during their lifetime. Men and women serve as representatives of God on earth. As quoted previously, God addresses men and women by saying:

> *"You are the best of people, evolved for mankind. Enjoining what is right, forbidding what is wrong, and believing in Allah." (Qur'an 3:110)*

---

[10] Qur'an, 1-2.

For man being God's representative, the Qur'an states:

"Behold, thy Lord said to the angels: 'I will create a vicegerent on earth'" (Qur'an 2:30)

And on man's responsibility, the Qur'an says:

"We indeed offer the trust to the heavens and the earth and the mountains; but they refused to undertake it, being afraid thereof: but man undertook it." (Qur'an 33:72)

When Allah refers to humanity as "mankind" or "people" or "O you who believe" and asks them to do well, this is a command for both sexes, not only just to men or to women. According to Islam, men and women in the social system are sisters and brothers to each other. This sisterhood and brotherhood is strengthened through faith alone. It is their faith that interconnects people and also makes them responsible socially, legally, and morally. Alluding to husbands and wives as garments to each other, God says:

"They are your garments and you are their garments."(Qur'an 2:187)

Garments in this context allude to mutual respect, dignity, completion, modesty, support and feedback, comfort, and protection from evil doing. It does not say that women are only comfort for men. In matrimony there is total equality in the relationship between a man and woman. This mutuality of love and respect, support and protection, dignity and modesty is established in this verse:

"And among His signs is this, that He created for you mates from among yourselves, that you may dwell in tranquility with them, and he has put love and mercy between your (hearts): verily, in that are signs for those who reflect."(Qur'an 30:21)

CREATION OF MANKIND

Muslims strongly believe that God is just and Absolute Just. If God is just, then discrimination in His creation will create doubt in His being just. Of course, there is a difference between discrimination and disparity. There are differences in creation that divide but that do not necessarily discriminate. Disparity does not discriminate; instead, it provides for natural growth and completion. The Qur'an is very clear about human creation:

> *"O mankind! Reverence your Guardian Lord, who created from a single soul, created of like nature, his mate, and from them twain scattered (like seeds) countless men and women—fear Allah, through whom you demand your mutual rights."(Qur'an 4:1)*

Praise the Lord for His justice. He has created men and women from the same soul and the same nature. When the Qur'an speaks of a "single soul," it means that in the creation of humanity, there is no duality or discrimination. Mankind is one mankind; men and women have been created from dry clay.

> *"He created man from sounding clay, from mud molded into shape."(Qur'an 15:26)*

It is important to note that the Arabic word *insan,* which has been translated as "man," or *annas,* which has been translated as "people," applies to both genders.

Dr. Farid Younos

There are many people, Muslims and non-Muslims who believe that women have been created from the left rib of man. This left-side creation has caused women worldwide to be second-class citizens. The above verse completely destroys the notion that women are created from the left or right side of man. As a matter of fact, in the history of Tabari, the most authentic history of Islam, there is no mention of right or left in the subject of human creation. When Allah placed Adam in paradise, he was alone without a spouse with whom he could seek peace and comfort. Adam slept for a while and when he awoke, sitting by his side was a woman that God had created from his rib.[11] The use of the word *rib,* however, is a misinterpretation of the language, which has caused women to be second-class citizens. "The translation 'rib' is incorrect, and the word so translated has the real meaning, in both Arabic and Hebrew, of 'nature, disposition, or constitution.' Eve, that is, woman, was created then out of the same nature or disposition as man. Since the word has been mistranslated as rib, the legend arose that woman was created from the left rib of Adam, and therefore all women are lacking one rib!"[12] The "logical" conclusion should be "man" is missing a rib! According to a dictum of Prophet Mohammad, woman was not created from man's rib but "represents his 'half twin.'"[13]

[11] Azudin, Ibn-Kathir. History of Tabari. Vol. I, pp. 34, Persian translation.
[12] Shari'ati, Ali. On the Sociology of Islam. Mizan Press, Berkeley, 1979.
[13] Boisard, Marcel A. Humanism in Islam. American Trust Publications, Indiana, 1988

From a biological point of view, the Qur'an clearly has verses about the nature of creation:

"Was (man) not a small quantity of sperm which has been poured out? After that, he was something which clings, then God fashioned him in due proportion."(Qur'an 75:37-38)

As stated earlier, man is part of nature and nature is part of man. The Qur'an supports this idea in the following verse:

"He [God] caused you to grow from the Earth."(Qur'an 11:61)

Also, it is said:

"We fashioned you from soil."(Qur'an 22:5)

These verses assist people to understand that God created humanity biologically, spiritually, and naturally from the same source: soul, water, and soil. These verses apply to both men and women. Also, having created mankind in the best form, Allah says:

"We have indeed created man in the best of moulds."(95:4)

"Best of moulds" means form, nature and constitution, and implies that both sexes have been given dignity and beauty. Therefore, God has not discriminated in His creation and both men and women are equal in creation.

MEN AND WOMEN IN SOCIETY

The first section, the creation of humanity, clearly reveals that men and women are created equal in the sight of Allah. This section deals with the role of Muslim men and women in society. This chapter will try to answer if men and women are equal in creation, are they also equal in society?

Islam came to redeem mankind, male or female, from any sort of servitude, exploitation, or slavery. To this idea, Allah, the Almighty, addressed mankind, saying:

"We have honored the children of Adam."(Qur'an 17:70)

Verse 17:70 means that Allah has given dignity and superiority to men and women over His creation. He gave mankind, male and female, responsible to obey God and to obey His Apostle, who is the best example of conduct for humanity. And He said:

"Obey Allah and obey the Messenger: but if you turn away he is only responsible for the duty placed on him and you for that placed on you. If you obey him, you shall be on right guidance. The Messenger's duty is only to preach the clear message."(Qur'an 24:54)

As He did regarding creation, the Almighty God who is Just, All Knowing, and All Wise, addressed men and women equally in society. He said:

> *"The Believers are but a single Brotherhood: so make peace and reconciliation between your two (contending) brothers; and fear Allah, that you may receive Mercy."(Qur'an 49:10)*

Two very important ideas in this verse need to be discussed. One is the concept of *ukhwa* (brotherhood) in Islam. In the Arabic language *ukhwa* can be applied to women as well as to men; thus, this verse alludes to the total sisterhood and brotherhood within the Muslim community. In this verse we see equal social justice between men and women.

The book of wisdom, the Qur'an, starts with the name of Allah and ends with the name of *annas* (people);[14] thus, there is a direct relationship between God and people, who are comprised of both males and females. God is the God of people; His book is the book of the people, regardless of their gender, race, color or social status. Men and women are bound by a triangle consisting of *aquida* (belief), *ilm* (knowledge), and *ammal* (work or action). Men and women reach Allah through pure belief, knowledge, and good work. After belief, the foundation of Islam is knowledge because *ilm* is the enlightenment of *aquida* and the backbone of *ammal.* In other words, a person has to believe in God first. His/her belief becomes stronger through knowledge. Once a person's belief system is polished, it goes into action. Knowledge is between

---

[14] Shariati, Ali. The collections of wirtings number 24. Persian text Ilham Publications, Tehran.

belief and action because it is knowledge that enlightens the belief; without knowledge the belief cannot work out as a social norm and value. Without proper knowledge belief would be vague and comprised of superstitions. Hence, all actions should be based on knowledge, and sound reasoning. God Almighty never discriminated between men and women in these three concepts. Everyone is entitled to

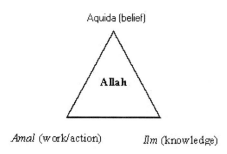

believe in Allah, to learn knowledge, and to try to apply knowledge to his/her everyday life. A person achieves prosperity in this world as well as in the hereafter through knowledge and its application.

The social role of men and women in society can be discussed in the following areas: Worship, World, Work, and War. World relations refer to the economic, social, political, and so forth interactions between men and women in the social system. An examination of the role of Muslim men and women in the light of the Qur'an and the *sunnah* (traditions) of the Prophet follows.

Worship:

As stated earlier, worship means the total acceptance of and obedience of God and His messenger. God created both sexes to complement each other, to fulfill God's mission on earth as His vicegerent, to support each other in good deeds, and worship only God. The Qur'an states:

"Thy Lord hath decreed that ye worship none but Him."(Qur'an 17:23)

Also God says:

"And stand before Allah in a devout (frame of mind.)"(Qur'an 2:238)

In another verse Allah commands mankind saying:

"O ye who believe! Give your response to (i.e., obey) Allah and His Messenger, when He calleth you to that which will give you life…."(Qur'an 8:24)

Men and women in Islam have the same and equal responsibility to carry on Allah's orders. Only in some areas, however, has a woman's responsibility been reduced due to their maternal responsibility, but this reduction of responsibility does not mean that women are unequal to men. As stated earlier, worship in Islam is to act on God's commands; therefore, all verses apply to both genders. For example, the Qur'an states:

> *"And be moderate in thy pace, and lower thy voice"(Qur'an 31:19)*

Here Allah addresses all humanity, men and women, not just men or not just women. In this verse He tells them to be moderate and to lower their voices when talking. It is important to realize that most verses in the Qur'an are universal in nature; they are not gender-focused at all. Some verses allude to men and sometimes to women; however, these cases depend on a particular situation and serve the purpose of providing a better clarification of Muslims' social status, morality, and character. The following verses are solid proof of the validity of this theory:

> *"And for those who launch a charge against their spouse…"(Qur'an24: 6)*

Verse 24:6 addresses both genders, not just men charging against their wives. The word *zwajahum* (or spouses as it is used in this verse) encompasses both husbands and wives. In the same *sura,* (chapter) Allah addresses both genders specifically mentioning their gender saying:

> *"Why did not the believers men and women."(Qur'an 24:12)*

In verses 31 and 32, Allah singles out men and women saying:

"Say to the believing men that they should lower their gaze and guard their modesty"(Qur'an 24:31)

And

"And say to the believing women that they should lower their gaze and guard their modesty"(Qur'an 24:32)

Praise God for His justice that He addresses both equally, enjoining them to be moral characters. Both men and women are responsible for their social conduct. All Muslims are responsible to Allah for their own morality and character. Islam does not deprive one gender at the expense of the other, and does not deprive women from social life to safeguard men's purity. The great *jihad* (struggle) is with the soul. The above two verses clearly show Allah's justice in the social system. Equality exists between both genders in society. Also, the above verses address men and women within the social system, and not at home. Therefore, since there was no seclusion of sexes during the time of the Prophet Mohammad, there is no seclusion of sexes in Islam.

The mosque plays a major role in Islamic life. It used to be the center of learning, decrees, academic gathering and spiritual exercises. In the time of the Prophet Mohammad, women stood behind men and performed prayers. Today, the majority of mosques have secluded women and made a separate room for them. This act is against the Islamic law that is derived from the Qur'an and the tradition of the Prophet. In early Islamic civil life men waited for women to leave the mosque first and then they would leave.[15]

According to one *Hadith,* men and women used to perform ablution together. [16] This tradition is extremely important in the study of social interaction between Muslim men and women. This *Hadith* reveals two concepts. First, that there is no such thing as seclusion between men and women. Secondly, the responsibility for proper conduct is placed upon each person's relationship with God and his/her own integrity. The responsibility to act properly is not in the hands of authorities such as the government. It is important to note that most *ulema* (men of knowledge in Islam) have interpreted this *hadith* as being only for husbands and wives. The *hadith*, however, does not specify any particular relationship between men and women but refers generally to men and women.

Haj of Ka'ba, a pilgrimage to the Ka'ba in Mecca, is another clear example of gender equality. Both genders worship Allah during the entire *Haj* period without any restriction. No *hadith* of the Prophet that demanding seclusion after the *Haj* ceremony could be found. It is important to bring up here that the role of the Islamic state is not to control moral values; rather, the role of the state is to promulgate proper education of and knowledge for the community. When members of a community understand their responsibility toward

---

[15] Al-Bukhari, The Book of Prayer, Volume 1, section 8, No 809

[16] Al-Bukhari, The Book of Ablution, Volume 1, section 4, chapter 45

their Creator, then of their own conscience, they will act morally without pressure.

World:

Knowledge:

The world of Muslim men and women begins with knowledge. Through knowledge men and women recognize their position and responsibility in social interaction. It was through the educational interaction of Aisha, the beloved wife of the Prophet, that the knowledge of hadith grew tremendously, and the Islamic culture developed as a strong code of social affairs.

According to one report, the Prophet Mohammad said that the first thing God created was the pen, [17] and the first word divinely revealed to the Prophet Mohammad was to "read." After acquiring *iman* (faith), knowledge lays the foundation of learning and education in Islam for both sexes. Hence, learning and education in Islam is extremely important because the Qur'an is the primary source of learning. God is the Eternal source of Wisdom and knowledge for Muslims. Mankind learns from Him what He has chosen to teach mankind. The Qur'an introduced Allah to us as:

---

[17] Tabari, Mohammed Bin Jarir, History of Tabari, volume 1, Persian text

> *"He who taught (the use of) the pen and taught man that which he knew not."(Qur'an 96:4&5)*

Since everything is learned from God, there is, according to Muslim lexicographers, a relation between the terms God and education. It is as follows:

"…the derivation of the term *'tarbiyah'* (education) occurs on several occasions. As a matter of fact, the terms *Rabb* (God) and *'tarbiyah'* are considered by Arab lexicographers to be derived from the same root. Maududi mentions that 'to educate and take care of' is one of the several meanings implicit in the term *Rabb.* Qurtubi says that the *rabb* is a description given to anyone who performs a thing in a complete manner. Razi makes a comparison between Allah the Educator and the human educator. He mentions that unlike the human educator, Allah the Educator knows well the needs of those who are being educated because He is their Creator. In addition to that His care is not limited to a certain group. He is concerned with educating all creatures; that is why He is described as *'Rabb al-Alamin.'"[18]

---

[18] Abdullah, Abdul Rahman Salih. Educational Theory: A Qur'anic Outlook, Umm Al-Qura University, Saudi Arabia, 1982

This quotation explains why Muslims believe that intelligence bonds men to God.

The Prophet Mohammad was a great promoter of knowledge. He said "Seek knowledge even in China"[19] and "Seek knowledge from cradle to grave."[20] In another *hadith*, the Prophet mentioned, "Learning is obligatory for all Muslims, men and women."[21]

In these sayings of the Prophet above, there are no gender preferences, but rather an equal consideration for both genders in learning and education. Several points can be drawn from the above quotations. The phrase, 'even in China' alludes to the idea that learning and education do not recognize borders. Knowledge is universal; and it should be grasped anytime, anywhere. The phrase, 'from cradle to grave' implies learning is a continuous never-ending process. Regardless of sex, a person should always be in the process of learning since this is a form of communication with Allah. The role of the Qur'an is "to give woman her rightful place in society, as basically the equal to man and to make Social Justice the very foundation for [a] healthy collective life"[22] This *Hadith* (saying of the Prophet) also eliminates the concept of age in relation to learning. Men and women should be in touch with the sources of knowledge throughout their entire lives;

---

[19] Al-Bukhari, Sahih Al-Bukhari, trans. Muhamad Muhsin Khan, vol.1, Book of Knowledge, Islamic University, Medina, 1981.

[20] Ibid.

[21] Ibid.

[22] Ansari, Fazl-ur-Rahman. The Qur'anic Foundations and Structure of Muslim Society. Vol.1, pp. xxiv-xxv. World Federation of Islamic Missions, Karachi, 1977.

otherwise, they lose the motivation for life, and their minds become stagnant. The third *Hadith* quoted above is extremely important because it eradicates any discrimination between the sexes. The education of both sexes brings cooperation, unity, and harmony in a social system. Inequity in intellectual levels within a family leads to a lack of communication and growth. God knows that without knowledge man, His vicegerent on earth cannot fulfill His mission. In order to know one's own soul and nature, a person has to seek knowledge. God asks man to pray for advancing knowledge as seen in the following verse.

"O my Lord! Advance me in knowledge"(Qur'an 20:114)

The purpose of education in Islam is twofold; each facet interrelates. One facet is the spiritual growth of man. Without spiritual achievement man will not recognize his social responsibility toward men; this responsibility is the second purpose of learning. The purpose of education in this life is to transform both men and women from a state of unconsciousness to that of consciousness. This transformation happens only by reaching God. The Prophet Mohammad said, "He who knows himself, knows his Lord."[23] Therefore, for both genders, social consciousness in Islam begins with knowing oneself. Education is meant to raise man to the intellectual level at which he/she would question and ask about the origin and the

---

[23] Mutahheri, Murtaza. Man and Universe, Ansaryian Publications: Iran, 1997.

purpose of his/her creation. By questioning, mankind establishes a communion with the Almighty Creator. This communion transforms knowledge into wisdom, which cannot be acquired by learning, but can be only divinely inspired.

When examining the Qur'an, all verses relating to learning and knowledge call upon both sexes. The following verses are solid reasons for educational equity between sexes:

"Only scholars will be able to reason it out" (Qur'an 29:43),

"Say: Those who know and those who don't, will they ever be equal" (Qur'an 39:9),

"Allah grants wisdom to whom He pleases; and whoever is so granted has been given a great good indeed. For only those with sharp minds will be able to grasp" (Qur'an 2:269).

The Prophet's wives, called um *al mumineen* (mother of the believers) are the role models for Islamic education. Abu Mussa, one of the Prophet's disciples, narrated that whenever Muslims had a problem, they would find the answer with Aisha.[24] Aisha is called The Teacher because she was a scholar of religion and the most knowledgeable person in

---

[24] Jamal, Ahmad M. .Zanane Barguzidah [Chosen Women] trans. By M. Hanif Balkhi from Arabic to Persian. Peshawar, 1374 of solar hijra.

judgment and religious opinion. Aisha reported a great number of the Prophet's sayings especially in the areas of relations between men and women and in domestic affairs. In fact, Aisha was the greatest muhadith (a scholar of Hadith) among women in her time. And that is why appropriately she was called The Teacher.[25] The respect with which she is regarded tells us that women in Islam have the same opportunity to learn and to propagate all branches of knowledge. Also, Fatima, the daughter of the Prophet was a role model of manners and knowledge in Islam. Aisha reported that she had not seen anyone more knowledgeable than Fatima except the Prophet. Aisha again reported that she has not seen anyone so close in manners and speaking to the Prophet than Fatima.[26] As the Prophet was a role model for the whole community, so were his family members that followed his example.

It is obvious through the direct study of the Qur'an and the tradition of the Prophet, that men and women in Islam have an equal access to knowledge. Additionally, learning and education are mandatory for both genders. Unfortunately, today, more women than men are uneducated and illiterate in Muslim societies. For example, under the rule of the Taliban in Afghanistan, women were deprived of an education, a practice that is against the Qur'an and the tradition of the Prophet. According to Ahmed Rashid, the author of *Taliban*, illiteracy was affecting 90% of girls and 60% of boys. With the arrival of the Taliban, the situation worsened. "The Taliban cancelled out years of effort

---

[25] Ibid.
[26] ibid.

by the Mujaheddin…to educate the population, by shutting down all girls' schools. Most boys' schools also closed as their teachers were women."[27] Ironically, no Muslim countries and their governments condemned these un-Islamic acts of the Taliban. The only exception was Iran, which issued this statement: "Through their fossilized policies the Taliban stop girls from attending school, stop women working out of their homes and all that in the name of Islam. What could be worse than committing violence, narrow-mindedness and limiting women's rights and defaming Islam."[28]

Politics:

In the time of Prophet Muhammad, and after that, women had a role and a voice in the political system of the *ummah* (Muslim community and social order). Indeed, the Qur'an gave this political right to men and women. Regarding women in politics, the Qur'an states:

> *"O Prophet! When believing women come to thee to take the oath of fealty to thee…then do thou receive their fealty, and pray to Allah for the forgiveness (of their sins): for Allah is*

---

[27] Rashid, Ahmed. "Taliban: Militant Islam, Oil and Fundamentalism in Central Asia." Yale University Press: New Haven, 2000, pg. 113.

[28] Ibid, 116.

Oft-Forgiving, Most Merciful." (Qur'an 60:12).

Verse 60:12 clearly indicate that women are participants in the socio-political systems, but this verse does not apply just for women at home; it includes women in society as well. Also, this verse reveals to us that women are part of the political decision-making process because it talks of *baia,'* an allegiance of women to the Prophet and also of the Prophet to them.

The historical story of a woman debating with Caliph (representative and head of state) Omar is another indication of women's role in the social and political systems. According to the story, a woman debated with Omar in the mosque and proved her point about women's dowries. She made Omar declare in front of everyone that he was wrong and she was right. (Badawi 1980:24) This important incident conveys several messages. First, women were knowledgeable enough to defend their rights according to the Qur'an without men helping them. Accordingly, in carrying the message of the Qur'an, women are equal to men. Second, women were present in the mosque and socially active, for as stated earlier, women prayed behind the men, not in seclusion. Third, this story conveys the message that all Muslim citizens in an Islamic state are equal in front of the law. Even a ruler like Omar if he were wrong, could not go against Islamic law. Fourth, the story shows the freedom of social interaction, social gathering, and freedom of speech regardless of gender.

There is a chapter in the Qur'an called *Al-Mujadilah*, which means "the woman who pleads." In the first verse Allah asks the Prophet, to listen to the argument raised by a woman concerning her husband:

> *"Allah has indeed heard (and accepted) the statement of the woman who pleads with thee concerning her husband and carries her complaint (in prayer) to Allah. And Allah (always) hears the arguments between both sides among you: for Allah hears and sees all things."(Qur'an 58:1).*

This verse tells Allah's justice encompasses both genders. Also, socially speaking, a woman is pleading with Allah for justice against a man. So well was her complaint received that a verse was revealed for the sake of that woman. Again, this incident demonstrates the respect for and rights given to women and positions both sexes equally in front of the law.

In March 628 AD, when Uthman ibn Affan (a disciple of the Prophet who later was appointed the Third Caliph) was dispatched on behalf of the Prophet, Umm Salamah, a female, played an important role after the signing of the Treaty of Hudaybah (a treaty of peace between the Prophet and the infidels of Quraish). Unhappy about this treaty, the Muslims ignored an order of the Prophet to sacrifice their animals. The Prophet went to Umm Salamah and told her of the problem. She asked the Prophet to sacrifice his camel first and then to cut his hair. The Prophet followed Umm Salamah's advice; then, the others followed his lead.[29] This story is very significant, for it shows even the Prophet of Islam consulted with his wives on social and political issues and followed their advice whenever it was in consonance with his principles. Therefore, this story of Umm Salamah shows the direct involvement of women in the social and political life of Islam.

Another historical event involving women in the political life of Islam concerns Aisha, the beloved wife of the Prophet. She wanted to take the revenge of Uthman, the third Caliph. After campaigning and attracting many supporters, staged a war called the *War of Jamal*. Umm Salamah disagreed with Aisha's plan and wrote a detailed letter to her, which Aisha rejected.[30] These stories did not occur because these women were the Prophet's wives; rather, these incidents occurred because women who were properly educated in Islam played a role on par with men in the social and political life of the *ummah.*

Social Interaction:

The deprivation of women in social life started after the era of the four righteous Caliphs. During the life of the Prophet, when the Islamic state was emerging as a political entity, both men and women contributed to its growth. For example, the first

---

[29] Hassan, Ibrahim Hassan. *Political History of Islam.* Translated into Persian by Kasem Paynda, 9th edition, 1376 AH (solar calendar), pg. 145.

[30] Ibid, 310.

munbar (pulpit) of the mosque was made at the suggestion of a woman. The story tells how the three-step pulpit came into existence. In the beginning, mosques did not have a pulpit. One day, when the Prophet, was standing and delivering his sermon, a woman, who had a slave who was a carpenter, asked the Prophet if she could make him something upon which to sit. The Prophet answered that if she pleased, she could do that.[31] Again we learn from this story that women sat in the mosque with their fellow brothers. Secondly, everyone had an opportunity to discuss the issues of the new Islamic society or system, to contribute to it, and be part of it. Third, men and women openly discussed their concerns with the Prophet Mohammad. This story illustrates how an Islamic society should be: It should have no biases or seclusion against women.

It is widely understood that after the Prophet, the *Imams* and the *ulema* would be the leaders of the community. As such, they should be role models for the Muslim people. The story of Hassan Basri and Raabia Adawia is a beautiful example of Muslim men and women sitting together without seclusion and chatting about knowledge. Hassan Basri narrates that one day, as he was chatting with Raabia on truth and the path of spirituality, it did not come to his mind that he was a man, and it did not come to her mind that she was a woman.[32] This story teaches that the top-notch

---

[31] Al-Bukhari, Sahih. *The Book of Prayer*, Hadith 440.
[32] Naishaapouri, Faridudin Ataar *Tazkratulawlia*. pg. 72, Trans. by Dr. Muhammad Istilami into Persian, Zawar Publication: Tehran, Iran, 1365 AH (solar calendar)..

awlia (friends of Allah) did not require seclusion between the sexes; instead, they were able to engage in open discussion. Since these friends of Allah are the role models for the Muslim community, all of society should also be allowed to interact without seclusion. Muslim men and women followed the tradition of the Prophet Mohammad; women were allowed and even encouraged to discuss, suggest, propose, and to receive their answers in the mosque. Historically, the only women who were rightfully secluded in Islam were the wives of the Prophet. In the Qur'an God asks that the Prophet's wives, not other women be secluded (Qur'an 33:32-33). Additionally, they were not allowed to remarry after the Prophet's death. This rule, however, does not apply to other Muslim men and women as is made clear by the story of Hassan Basri.

The calendar of Islam starts with *Hijrah*, the migration of Prophet Mohammad, from Mecca to Yathrib. (To highlight both emigration and the emigrant, after the Prophet's migration there, upon the Hijrah, Yathrib was renamed Madina, which is short for Madinatul Nabi 'the city of the Prophet'.) This migration marks the turning point in the history of Islam. First of all, both men and women migrated together. Secondly, migration changed the worldview of Muslims from that of a tribal attitude to that of a civilized, metropolitan outlook. For this reason, Yathrib was renamed Madina, which means the "city." In a city, both men and women contribute equally to the civilization of Islam. According to the history of *tabari*, migration was the distance between truth and falsehood.

When dealing with social interaction, another story of the Prophet comes to mind. The Prophet granted the leadership of Bani Qariza to Saad ibn Moaaz. In the War of the Trench, when Saad was injured, the Prophet said that he should be taken to the tent of Rafida, a Muslim woman, so that she could take care of him.[33] All of these stories tell us that women are an integral part of an Islamic society. Both genders have contributed to making Islam a world civilization.

Hijab:

Hijab is a dignified and modest way of dressing. *Hijab* is not a uniform, and nowhere in the Qur'an or in the hadith of the Prophet Mohammad do we find a specification defining a dress; both men and women should wear proper clothing. Men's *awrah* (those places that are not permissible to be seen) goes from the navel to the knee while women's *awrah* covers the whole body except the face, the hands, and the feet. *Hijab* prohibits see-through material and requires that the whole body be covered properly with hands and face open. According to several *Ahadith,* the veil is not required because a woman like a man should be able to communicate in the market and carry items easily with her hands. In fact, during the *tawaf* (circumambulation) in the *Ka'ba,* women are required to keep their faces uncovered. A woman's dress should be comfortable

---

[33] Tabari, Muhammad ibn Jarir. *The History of Tabari.* Vol. 3, pg. 1087, Trans. by Kasam Paynda into Persian, Asatir Publication: Tehran, Iran, 1368 AH (solar calendar).

enough not to become an obstacle for her activities and should also cover her *zina* (bodily beauty) properly. Again, a story involving the Prophet proves this point. A woman approached the Prophet Mohammad asking if she could perform Hajj on behalf of her father. The Prophet answered that she could. The woman did not have a veil and communicated with the Prophet with modesty and integrity. If a veil were required, he would have objected to her request.[34]

In his well-known book, *Humanism in Islam,* Professor Boisard writes:

"There is nothing Islamic about wearing the veil which materially illustrates the inferiority of the Muslim woman. Muhammad recommended only that they behave in a modest fashion and that they cover their hair and necks with a scarf. It was apparently in Persia and the Near East that Islam encountered this custom in the cities. The Muslims adopted it for psychological and social reasons, since in those days a woman who showed her face had the reputation of loose morals. This practice was maintained for a long time under the pressure of tradition, not through any religious obligation."[35]

Muslim men and women are required by Allah to live with dignity and integrity. For this reason, the

---

[34] Siddiqi, M. Mazheruddin *Women in Islam.* Adam Publishers and Distributors: New Delhi, 1980, pg. 106.

Qur'an addresses both genders telling them not to become involved in any sort of immoral act, but to keep their chastity. The Qur'an says:

> *"So the believing men, they should lower their gaze and guard their modesty, that will make for greater purity for them and Allah is well acquainted with all that they do.*
>
> *And so the believing women, they should lower their gaze and guard their modesty that they should not display their beauty and ornaments except what (must ordinarily) appear thereof…"(24:30-31).*

Many scholars have written about verses 24:30-31. Here follows an analysis. First of all, this verse does not mean that men and women should be in segregation. On the contrary, they can be together in society while living with modesty and mutual respect. When communicating with the opposite sex, the parties should not look at each other straight in the eyes, as is common practice in the West. It is not necessary to have eye contact when having an open and serious business communication. Second, this verse applies to men and women in society, not to a family. If Allah had wanted men and women to be segregated, He would have commanded it.

Islam is a way of life that protects human dignity. Men and women dressing properly constitute one part of this dignity as established by the Qur'an and the traditions of the Prophet Mohammad. For example, it is recommended that women wear a proper dress and cover their beauty. Also, the Prophet Mohammad recommended that men should avoid wearing gold ornaments and silk clothes. Conversely, women are allowed to wear gold as well as silk garments. Women are mothers of believers, and their position is so high in society as well as in the family that the Prophet Mohammad said, "Paradise is under the foot of the mothers." By stating, "Women are queens of their home," the Prophet revealed that wives are equal to their husbands. With such praise Islam does not want women to become sex objects in society. Like men, women need to be respected and admired, not because of their beauty, but because of their talent, knowledge, and Islamic piety. Therefore, when a woman dresses improperly, she shows her lack of faith to the Qur'an and to the leadership of the Prophet, for she is not portraying Islamic values. Islamic values recommend that a woman be covered, not that she isolates herself from the rest of society. In fact, dressing properly allows her to interact freely. In this way everyone will respect her and look at her as a distinguished individual rather than as an object of lust and passion. Dress symbolizes the personality of an individual. Seeing a woman with a white dress and a cap identifies her as a nurse. Seeing a woman in a business suit and an attaché case under her arm identifies her as a businesswoman or a lawyer. By the same token, a woman dressed half-naked and provocatively on the street of any big city identifies her as a prostitute. On the other hand, a woman in *hijab* is immediately identified as a person of faith, principle and dignity. Women who believe in the Islamic faith do not provide an opportunity to provoke passion in weak men, which will injure their character and personality.

Secular-minded Muslim women object to *hijab* claiming that they should not be judged because of their dress. These women, who do not desire to wear *hijab*, say that Islam is not fair to require them were such apparel. Furthermore, they claim that men should have the proper moral character to not view women with a passionate eye. Thus, these secular Muslim women place the moral problem on the men rather than on themselves.

There are several points to be made concerning these arguments by secular-minded women. I have to agree with the second part of their complaint: men in society should control their attitudes and desires, and the Qur'an commands them to lower their eyes. This does not, however, justify women not dressing as the Qur'an decrees. A Muslim woman should know the real definition of picty. Picty is simply fearing Allah and obeying His orders. A pious woman always tries to follow the footsteps of the Prophet Mohammad, just as her counterpart, a pious man, follows his footsteps. At this stage, the equality of gender takes shape according to the command of Allah.

In terms of equality between the genders, men and women need to be studied physiologically and anatomically. As stated earlier, men and women complement each other. Both genders have different qualities to complete the other. For example, a battery must have a positive and a negative side in order to work; two positive or two negative sides could not work together in order to give power. Hence, the two different charges complement each other; each is equally important in achieving their purpose. By the same token, men and women have physiological and anatomical qualities to achieve their completion. These qualities are equal. In the same regard, some of the laws that apply to a man's and woman's physical and emotional differences might not be the same, but they are equal in their purpose and goal. The purpose of these laws is to allow free social interaction between men and women without creating unnecessary desires and without causing a chaotic atmosphere. Keep in mind that in Islam the ultimate goal is *jannah* (paradise). In order to achieve *jannah,* Islam dictates the proper conduct and dress for an individual. The dress must correspond to the nature of a man and a woman. Despite the fact that men and women are created from the same soul, the natural forces within the soul are from the wisdom of Allah. In order to avert chaos and desires, the dress of one gender must match the physical characteristics of that gender and the emotional characteristics of the opposite sex. This real application and meaning of Islam brings peace to both genders. *Hijab* in the context of social interaction must bring peace and harmony. Men of wisdom say that men are slaves of passion while women are slaves of compassion. This is natural law. To overcome a man's passion and the emotional characteristics of man, a woman's dress must be as modest as the hijab. Though the dress code is not the same for the genders, the code fulfills equal results; thus, the code is fair.

Witnessing:

One of the major misconceptions about gender equality stems from the verse of surah Al-Baqarah (The Hiefer), the second chapter of the Qur'an, which is often quoted as discriminating between men and women in the realm of testimony. For the purpose of this analysis, we quote the relevant part of the verse in question:

"Oh ye who believe, when ye deal with each other, in transactions involving future obligations in a fixed period of time…get two witnesses, out of your own men, and if there are not two men, then a man and two women, such as ye choose, for witnesses, so that if one of them errs, the other can remind her…"(Qur'an 2:182).

It needs to be mentioned that some interpreters ignored this verse in the light of gender equality while others gave a sometimes-confusing analysis. Others showed that this rule was made because of women's lack of education in the time of the Prophet. Still others have claimed that because of women's emotional mentality, they may make mistakes or become forgetful. All of these explanations, however, violate the principles of justice and equality between genders in Islam.

In order to understand the wisdom of Allah, witnessing must be examined in the light of science, or human psychology. Physiologically, men's brains on average are larger than women's. The Intelligence

Quotient (IQ) of men and women, however, is the same. Hence, this difference in brain size must indicate a difference in the way the genders think, not overall ability.[36] For this reason, verse 2:182 cannot be a discriminatory rule based on cognitive ability between genders.

Some psychological studies are important for our study. It is important to note, "While men and women can solve problems equally well, their approach and their process are often quite different."[37] Therefore, if one female witness replaced one of the male witnesses their different natures would cause clashes in their collaboration.

Secondly, women like to solve problems through discussion. Their preference for discussion results from women's emotional nature as it provides "an opportunity to explore, deepen or strengthen the relationship with the person they are talking with."[38] According to Judy B. Rosener's research published in the *Harvard Business Review,* women "encourage participation, share power and information, enhance other people's self worth, and get others excited about their work."[39] On the other hand, "for most men,

---

[36] Dr. Ruben Gur. Radio broadcast: "Men, Women and the Brain." Produced by WETA, Washington DC.

[37] Conner, Michael G., Psy.D. Clinical & Medical Psychologist. *Understanding The Difference Between Men And* *Women.*
http://www.oregoncounseling.org/ArticlesPapers/Documents/Differences MenWomen.htm

[38] Ibid.

[39] Rosener, Judy B. "Ways Women Lead." *Harvard Business Review*. Nov. 1, 1990.

solving a problem presents an opportunity to demonstrate their competence, their strength of resolve, and their commitment to a relationship."[40] Therefore, psychologically, men think and work more independently than women. Having two female witnesses in place of one male witness makes sense in light of their proclivity toward group interactions. The following psychological experiment aptly demonstrates this principle:

"Some of the more important differences can be illustrated by observing groups of young teenage boys and groups of young teenage girls when they attempt to find their way out of a maze. A group of boys generally establish a hierarchy or chain of command with a leader who emerges on his own or through demonstrations of ability and power. Boys explore the maze using scouts while remaining in distant proximity to each other. Groups of girls tend to explore the maze together as a group without establishing a clear or dominant leader. Relationships tend to be co-equal. Girls tend to elicit discussion and employ "collective intelligence" to the task of discovering a way out. Girls tend to work their way through the maze as a group. Boys tend to search and

---

[40] Conner, Michael G., Psy.D. Clinical & Medical Psychologist. *Understanding The Difference Between Men And Women.*
http://www.oregoncounseling.org/ArticlesPapers/Documents/Differences MenWomen.htm

explore using structured links and a chain of command."[41]

Another important psychological aspect is that "men have a tendency to dominate and to assume authority in a problem solving process."[42] Furthermore, they "do not attend well to the quality of the relationship while solving problems."[43] Following this reasoning, if there were one male and one female witness, the male witness would be likely to dominate the discussion and decision making; hence the male could bias the witnessing. Such a result would be unjust and therefore against the teachings of Islam.

Women also have emotional conflicts between their personal lives and witnessing. It has been shown that "women are prone to become overwhelmed with complexities that 'exist', or might exist, and might have difficulty separating their personal experience from problems."[44] Men on the other hand, "have an enhanced ability to separate themselves from problems and minimize the complexity that may exist."[45] In order to avoid such issues, it is logical and just to have two females witnessing together so that their personal experiences do not bias their judgment.

Furthermore, those women in the peri-menopause period, defined as "the two- to eight-year time period before menopause and the first year after the last

---

[41] Ibid.
[42] Ibid.
[43] Ibid.
[44] Ibid.
[45] Ibid.

menstruation," suffer many symptoms, including memory loss.[46] Women who are still menstruating also experience Premenstrual Syndrome (P.M.S.). P.M.S. causes many physical effects, which include difficulty concentrating.[47] Hence, in order to avoid any misjudgments and to maintain justice, which is the primary objective of Islam, two female witnesses are needed. Requiring two female witnesses is neither discriminatory against gender nor prejudicial, but simply a physiological phenomenon that must be taken into account for the sake of fairness.

Before ending this section, it is important to note that the verse 2:182 demonstrates the role women play in the social system, and in particular, in the judicial system. As long as women are properly dressed and act with modesty, they can participate in such matters alongside men. This also means that the seclusion of females has no place within the judicial system of Islam or in Islamic culture in general.

Work:

Three issues need to be discussed about employment within the Islamic society. First, is it permissible to employ women in the work force? Second, if it is permissible to do so, are women equal

---

[46]

http://www.pamf.org/health/toyourhealth/menopause.html
[47]

http://www.medformation.com/mf/stay.nsf/AdultTreatment/
Premenstrual_Syndrome

to men according to the Qur'an? Third, what are the limitations for both sexes?

As noted earlier, the Qur'an treats men and women equally. Concerning work, the Qur'an states for both sexes:

> *"Never will I suffer to be lost the work of any of you, be male or female. Ye are members, one of another."(Qur'an 3:195)*

The Arabic word for work is *a'mal*. Most interpreters of the Qur'an have interpreted verse 3:195 as a way to perform good deeds not for employment. Women are an integral part of an Islamic system including the workforce. Without their participation, society would be stagnant. According to 3:195, employment is permissible and also equally acceptable for both sexes.

According to the tradition of the Prophet, no ruling exists forbidding women to seek employment. If an Islamic government prohibits women from working, that government has violated the *shari'a* (Islamic Law). In the time of Prophet Mohammad, women worked and engaged in different trades.

The *hadith* of the Prophet, which alludes to the market as a place of evil temptations, could apply to both genders. In the market, people can lie, cheat, and commit fraud for the purpose of profit. These characteristics have nothing to do with gender since a man as well as a woman is just as liable to cheat when trading. Both genders can act immorally. It is so difficult to understand that in most writings, without any *Hadith* justification, scholars play down the psychological well-being, and intelligence of women.

Also, it is very wrong to compare Muslim men and women to Western men and women in the work force. As mentioned earlier, Muslim men and women are responsible ethically to Allah; people in the West, with all due respect, do not have that notion. In Western culture, talking about God goes against company policy. Once I said to an employee, "God bless you," which is a very common expression even in the West. The next morning, my boss called me in and said that someone was reported that I was propagating my religion. In the West even those who have faith and are churchgoers, do not often dwell on the idea that God sees them and hears them at all times. The definition of morality differs in the extreme between Muslim and Western cultures. "For the Muslim, the rule of conduct is the divine will, expressed in the Qur'an and made explicit by Muhammad's prophetic mission. It would be a grave error not to emphasize the eminently and fundamentally precise religious nature of these rules which determine the behavior of the Muslim."[48]

Before the Soviet invasion of Afghanistan, when I was in Kabul, men and women were working in the capital. These working relationships were just a sisterhood and brotherhood relationship; everyone knew how to behave with one another. We greeted each other saying "Sister" or "Brother." We behaved this way because the majority of Afghans follow the most liberal school of thought of Abu Hanifa. As a

---

[48] Boisard, Marcel A. *Humanism in Islam*. P.10, American Trust publication, 1988.

matter of fact, according to the Hanafi school of thought, women can be appointed judges.[49] The Taliban were different. They claimed to follow Abu Hanifa's school of thought but actually did not.

There are limitations of employment for both sexes in Islam. Since both genders are responsible to Allah when conducting business, neither men nor women are allowed to engage in unethical transactions. Both genders are responsible for establishing fair prices and are ethically responsible to treat their employees with dignity and respect. Also, both genders should have a sound mental attitude when entering the business world. Women have one extra limitation if they are mothers and have the responsibility of their children. In that case, the woman's primary responsibility is her children, not outside employment. If the children are responsible enough to take care of their daily routines, then with the agreement of her husband, the woman can seek employment:

There are different reasons that today's women seek employment:

1. In today's economic world, the incomes of most families are not adequate enough to make ends meet. This is true especially in the West where Muslims live in a consumer society. In this case, employment is not a choice but a necessity. In the developing Eastern countries though, which are not consumer societies, the

---

[49] Mujaddidi, Fazl-Ghani. *Dar Nizam Dawlat islami*. [The system of the Islamic state] Persian text. Enterprise printing Graphic, USA 1996.

actual income of the husband is not sufficient to support his family.

2. There are women who do not have the responsibility of a child or children, and they would like to be socially active as are many Muslim women in the West.

3. Highly educated women want to use their talents and expertise.

4. With today's technology women do not have much to do at home; machines do almost everything.

5. Nowadays, women in their late thirties or forties want to marry, but they feel that they are not young enough to raise a child, or sometimes the husband does not want a child. Demographically speaking, not wanting to have a child or having only one or two children is becoming common among Muslims because of a variety of socio-economic factors. Not withstanding their desires, this is, of course, in the hands of Allah.

6. There are some couples who cannot have a child naturally; these women want to work. The couple loves each other, and their intimate relationship is more important than having a child.

7. There are women and men who cannot find the right spouse, and they remain single. (Marriage is an important tradition of the Prophet providing that both agree to that wedlock. No one can marry a young virgin girl, a widow, or a divorcee without her permission.)[50] These women want to work.

It has been traditionally believed that women are not suitable for leadership because of their responsibilities as mothers and because their emotional attitudes as females might prevent them from making sound judgments. As shown in the earlier instances discussed above where women played a major role in politics, this way of thinking proved wrong. There is, however, a difference between *Imamat* and being the head of government. In *Imamat*, (religious leadership) the *Imam* leads the prayers. The head of government is not required to lead the prayer and does not send out religious decrees. The Hadith that rules out women leadership is referred to as *Imamat*. There is no such ruling according to any *Hadith* that women cannot be an administrator or the head of government. One *Hadith* indicates, "Never will such a nation succeed as makes a woman their ruler"[51] In this regard, Dr. Jamal Badawi has given a very understandable and reasonable illustration:

---

[50] Al Bukhari, shih. Book of Wedlock, vol.7, pp. 50-51, Trans.M.Muhsin Khan. Islamic University, Medina 1981
[51] Al Bukhari, SahihTrans. M.Muhsin Khan. vol.9, pp.170 Islamic University, Medina,1981

"While this hadith has been commonly interpreted to exclude women from the headship of states, other scholars do not agree with that interpretation. The Persian rulers at the time of the Prophet (P) showed enmity toward the Prophet (P) and toward his messenger [message] to them. The Prophet's response to this news may have been a statement about the impending doom of that unjust empire, which did take place later, and not about the issue of gender as it relates to headship of the state in itself"[52] (Badawi: 1999, P.39)

Employment of women is not a new issue. Omar ibn Khatab, the Second Caliph (head of state) of Islam, appointed a woman, Um Al –Shaifaa' bint Abdullah, as the marketplace supervisor. Dr. Badawi writes that this is "a position that is equivalent in our time to that 'Director of the consumer protection department.'"[53]

The Prophet of Islam consulted women in the affairs of state.[54] The research by Mujaddidi shows that women in the history of Islam were involved in the police department, city hall, and intelligence services. Women play an integral part of the Muslim society and are allowed to work based upon consultation with their

---

[52] Badawi, Jamal. Gender Equity in Islam. American Trust Publication, P.39, Indiana 1999.
[53] Ibid, p.19
[54] Mujaddidi, Fazl-Ghani. *Dar Nizam dawlat Islami* [The system of the Islamic state]. Persian text, Enterprise Printing Graphics, USA 1996.

husbands and their need to work if they do not have small children to take care of.

Another limitation for both sexes occurs when either men or women are outnumbered by the other gender in an organization. In either case, some degree of equity in numbers must be sought. Some scholars mention this only if men are outnumbered, but the matter of fact is if one genders surpasses the other, there is no ethical working condition. This qualification does not apply to highly professional, career-oriented fields such as medicine or business, only to blue-collar type jobs.

As noted in the case of a woman in Omar's time, it is permissible for both sexes to serve as bosses. When a male or female boss counsels an employee however, it must be in the presence of another official individual. The counseling of a female employee by a male employee or vice versa is not ethical in most work environments. Professors are the exception because in Islam, professors are role models of character and ethical values as they are *aalims,* or men of knowledge. Society's expectation of them, and their training, and their work environment make a professor's situation totally different than that of a company manager.

The bottom line is that nowadays, Muslim girls are studying at the universities alongside their brothers. These females have different expectations, and some even compete with their brothers. This situation cannot be ignored. There are some Muslim couples in America who are both professors and are even in the same department. Ibn Abas said, *"Al Qur'an, ufasserul zamaan*,"[55] which means that the Qur'an interprets itself according to the time in which we live. Times have changed and scholars have to make necessary changes without violating the principles of the Qur'an and the *sunnah*. Many youth do not think that Islam meets their needs in this day and age; therefore, they are not interested in Islam as a way of life or as a way of thinking and education. These youth are attracted to Western values because our *ulema* (men of knowledge) ignore both the youth as well as the present-day world. (For a very good discussion of this issue, please see *Islamization of Knowledge* by the late Dr. Al Faruqi).

Islam has never insisted on a rigid way of life. It has treated everyone equally; the rights of all Muslims, male and female, are equal before the law. Boisard writes:

> "The principle of equality is the cornerstone of the Islamic edifice; it has fashioned the construction thereof. History clearly shows that Islam managed to develop a homogenous and integrated society without classes, in which the claim of 'liberty, equality, and fraternity' (the main motivations of the revolts of the West) could not have stirred up true feelings since it did not fulfill a real need. The basic principle of the absolute equality of all men brings into focus the other two terms of the slogan –

---

[55] Tafisr Namouna, Persian text, vol.1 introduction, p. 20, 1377 of solar calendar, Tehran, Iran.

fraternity and liberty – by encompassing or, more exactly, transcending them."[56]

Unfortunately, our youth nowadays look to the West to find equality and justice! I interviewed eighteen young girls between the ages of sixteen and nineteen. I asked them if they would like to live in an Islamic country or the United States. Unanimously, they want to live in the United States. They think that in an Islamic country they would not be allowed to drive; they would not be allowed to work; they would not be allowed to choose the profession they wanted. All these young girls are practicing Muslims, who wore *hijab*, and are proud to be Muslims. Obviously, Islam has a great challenge. This challenge can be dealt with only if we change our faulty biases. As the Qur'an says:

> **"Allah will not change the fate of a people until they change what is in themselves"(Qur'an13: 11)**

The late Dr. Al Faruqi has written about verse 13:11 that change "is an absolute law of history."[57]

Furthermore, the hadith quoted about the exclusion of women from leadership positions is in direct contradiction to the text of the Qur'an where we read:

---

[56] Boisard, Marcel A. *Humanism in Islam*, pp.77-78. American Trust Publication, 1988

[57] Al Faruqi, Ismail R. Islamization of knowledge, (preface) International Institute of Islamic Thought, Herdon, 1987

"Let there arise out of you a band of people inviting to all that is good, enjoining what is right, and forbidding what is wrong: They are the ones to attain felicity." (Qur'an 3:104)

Verse 3:104 is the basis of Islamic government and leadership. It is very clear that the word *ummah* (Muslim community) has been used for inviting good and forbidding evil. Gender is not an issue according to this verse. All Muslims, male and female, are entitled to conduct the affairs of the community. To propagate good actions and to forbid evil is mandatory for all Muslims, male and female.

War:

Fourteen hundred years ago, the Islamic state established such an equal relationship among its members that the defense of Islam becomes an obligation for both genders. All verses concerning jihad and protection of the *ummah* relate to both males and females. Women not only assisted their brothers physically during the war, but also financially by means of alms contributed to strengthening the Islamic State.[58] The Prophet encouraged women to participate in good deeds of social affairs as well as religious

---

[58] Al Bukhari, Sahih. Vol. 2, The book of festivals, pp. 50-51. Trans. M. Mohsin Khan. Islamic University, Medina, 1981.

gatherings.[59] Women, alongside their Muslims brothers, played a major role in nation building. The defense of the Islamic faith and nation was as much a responsibility of men as of women. Allah says:

"Allah hath purchased of the believers their persons and their goods; for theirs (in return) is the Garden (of Paradise): They fight in His cause, and slay and are slain: A promise binding on Him in truth, through the Law, the Gospel, and the Qur'an: And who is more faithful to his Covenant than Allah? Then rejoice in the bargain which ye have concluded: That is the achievement supreme." (Qur'an 9:111)

In 9:111 Allah made both genders responsible for the noble cause – fighting for His cause. Allah scrutinizes both genders for their faithfulness. It was on the basis of this socio-political responsibility that women alongside men participated in the defense if Islam. In Al Bukhari, chapter 3, the Book of Jihad, it clearly mentions both men and women participated in jihad and martyrdom. Aisha, the Prophet's wife, participated along with *um Sulaim* in the battle of *Uhud*, by carrying water skins for the *mujahiddin* on her back.[60] Other women treated men who were

---

[59] Ibid.

[60] Al Bukhari, Shih. The book of Jihad, Vol. 4, chapter 65, pp. 83-86. Trans. M. Mohsin khan. Islamic University, Medina, 1981.

injured during the war, and some women supplied food and water to their Muslim brothers.[61]

These scenarios disclose that women are a vital part of the Islamic community. They are not just mothers or mistresses. Women can also bear social and political responsibilities as the need or desire arises.

---

[61] Ibid.

MEN AND WOMEN IN THE FAMILY

This chapter discusses whether or not Islam treats men and women equally in the family. The family relationship in Islam is extremely important because family has been called the small society. The family encompasses leadership, money management, nurturing, and education. In addition, the family unit is responsible for instilling Islamic values that emphasize oneness in all aspects of life. These values will continue into the next generation.

Men and Women are Equal in the Family:

Contrary to what people think about Islamic life and what is often heard, it is false that women hold a lower position than men. Concerning the relationship between a man and a woman, the Qur'an plainly states:

"They are your garments and you are their garments."(Qur'an2:187)

Once again, 2:187 shows the total equality between husband and wife in the family. One Hadith of the Prophet regarding the leadership and relationship within the household states, "Verily everyone of you is a shepherd and every one of you is responsible for his flock. The *Amir* (leader) is a shepherd over his people and shall be questioned about his subjects. A man is a shepherd over the members of his family and shall be questioned about them. A women is guardian over her household and shall be questioned as to how she managed the household."[62] Therefore, both the verse and the Hadith support the idea of equality.

There is a widespread misunderstanding of the word *qiwamah* and *daraja*. Dr. Badawi writes in his book *Gender Equity in Islam*, "no where does the Qur'an state that one gender is superior to the other. Some interpreters of the Qur'an mistakenly translate the Arabic word *qiwamah* (responsibility for the family) with the English word "'superiority.'" The Qur'an makes it clear that the sole basis for the superiority of any person over another is piety and righteousness, not gender, color or nationality."[63] A *daraja* has been translated in English as "degree" and the verse 228 of Sura Bakarah says,

"And men are a degree above them."

"Degree" in this context is not a matter of superiority of men and women but an economic responsibility of men towards women. In his interpretation of the verse, Abdullah Yusuf Ali writes, "The difference in economic position between the sexes makes the man's rights and liabilities a little greater than the woman's. Q. 4:34 refers to the duty of the man to maintain the woman, and to a certain difference in nature between the sexes. Subject to this, the sexes are on terms of equality in law, and in certain matters the physically weaker sex is entitled to special protection."

---

[62] Sahih Muslim, Collection of
[63] pg 13

It is important to note that in Islam, men and women are responsible to God as well as for their own moral character and self-consciousness—not to the autocracy of government. After studying the role of government in the time of the Prophet and the four Caliphs, it is obvious the government played a minimal role in controlling people's character and behavior. As long as people did not disturb the welfare of others and did not commit shameful acts in public, they were free to live as they wished. The story of Caliph Omar and a citizen of Madina is a case in point. It has been narrated that Caliph Omar patrolled in the evening to make sure everyone was safe, and to insure tranquility in the city. One night, he heard the sound of music coming from a house, and he entered the house from the back yard via the roof to find out what was going on in the house. He witnessed a man and a woman drinking wine and enjoying themselves. Omar, who had a hot temper, addressed the man saying "''O enemy of God! Do you think that Allah would forgive such a sin? The man answered: O Amir al Muminin! Do not rush to conclusions. If I have committed one sin, you have committed three of them. God Almighty tells you 'and spy not on each other,' you were spying; and He said, 'Enter houses through the proper doors', and you entered via the roof. And He said, 'O you who believe! Enter not houses other than your own, until you have asked permission and saluted those in them', you have entered without permission and you did not greet us.' Omar replied: 'If I forgive you, will you repent?' The man responded: 'Yes, if you forgive me, I will repent.''

Omar, the Caliph of Islam forgave that man and he repented."[64]

There are many rich maxims in this story for the Muslim community today. One is the honorable attitude of both the citizen and the ruler. Justice was done through the fear of God, and not through political leadership. People are entitled to have privacy. Both citizens and rulers are accountable only to God. Nowadays, houses are deliberately searched, and people are deliberately tortured to make them better Muslims. Islam did not spread through torture and force but through mercy and forgiveness.

Wedlock (Nikah):

Family life in Islam starts with *nikah,* which literally means a contract. Actually, wedlock in Islam is a social contract, not a sacred matrimony. Also, it is a virtuous social contract because it is based on Islamic law, derived from the Qur'an and the tradition of the Prophet. Since Muslims in the East or in the West could go to city hall and become husband and wife, why should Muslims perform wedlock per Islam?

According to Islam, we are all born Muslims and we need to live by the Islamic law and leave this world as Muslims. Therefore, the first reason of wedlock is to enforce the Islamic law in the land. Second, men and women complement each other. No man grows spiritually if there is no woman beside him, and no

---

[64] Al-Ghazali, Abu Hamed, Alchemy of Welfare, Volume 1.

woman will grow spiritually if there is no man beside her. According to the Qui'an, they are each other's garments. Wedlock is a *sunnah* of the Prophet. Because marriage is the foundation of the Islamic family, he placed much emphasis for the *ummah* (Muslim community) to marry. Third, within the Islamic belief system, no righteous child will be born without wedlock.[65] This righteousness is not a matter of moral character, but recognition of *tawhid* and the oneness of God. Fourth, a man and a woman are not permitted to associate with each other unless they are married. There is a moral virtue, and social responsibility in marriage, besides becoming *halal* (permissible) to each other. Marriage of the believers eradicates any sort of corruption within society such as adultery and fornication.

There are three aspects of the wedlock procedure:

1. **Witnesses:** Two witnesses are sufficient to witness a marriage. They need to know both parties very well and need to know that each is mentally sound and an adult. These witnesses should witness based upon their knowledge of the two that they are mentally sound for marriage and that neither of them has any mental problem that would be an obstacle for their married life. They would also bear witness in the future if a divorce takes place. The witnesses should witness that the woman is not married to anyone else. It is important that the age of the witness is close to that of the bride

---

[65] Ibid.

and the groom and the witness live near them. Of course, nowadays, people record their marriage, but witnesses are the most important characteristic of Islamic marriage and it is the tradition of the Prophet.

2. **Proposal and acceptance:** Both parties should have an equal opportunity to accept each other. Particularly in the case of a woman, no one should force her to marry someone without her permission. She can lay down any condition other than her dowry *(mahr)*. Her conditions must be according to Islamic law, not baseless conditions and desires, and all are subject to approval by the man. For example, it is a lawful condition for a woman to say at her wedding that she agrees to marry the man as long as he is not married to another woman. Or a woman can say that she will marry him if he provides a servant or a cook. But a woman cannot say as one of her conditions that she will not pray. This is not a lawful condition. The man can either accepts or reject the woman's conditions and has the right to lay down some conditions before the wedlock. Again, his conditions are subject to approval by the woman. Always, the conditions must be according to the Islamic law. This proposal and acceptance is a sort of open communication between the two before they commit to marriage. It is permissible for men and women to communicate in private in

the presence of others.[66] Please also refer to Sahih Bukhari, volume 7, and the Book of Wedlock, page 118. Both parties should utter three times that they accept each other. Out of modesty and respect for women, if the woman says it only one time or she is silent, according to the tradition of the Prophet, it is acceptable to consider this as an affirmation.

3. **Sermon:** The third part of the marriage ceremony is reciting or delivering a sermon. The wedding sermon must be in Arabic. There is no specific sermon or verse, but the verses recited should be related to family life and marriage. The one who officiates at the wedding can translate the verses into any other language after it is recited in Arabic. The following verses are common to recite in the wedding ceremony:

O mankind! Reverence your Guardian Lord, who created you from a single soul, created, of like nature, his mate, and from them twin scattered (like seeds) countless men and women—fear Allah, through whom ye demand your mutual (rights), (reverence) the wombs (that bore you): for Allah ever watches over you. (Al Nisa, 1)

---

[66] Younos, M. Farid. *Didar jawanaan kabl az nikaht* [the seeing of youth before nikah] in Persian. Caravan Monthly, California. Number 52, February 1998.

> *It is He Who has created man from water:*
> *Then has He established relationship of*
> *lineage and marriage: for thy Lord has power*
> *(over all things). (Al Furqan, 54)*
>
> *And among His signs is this, that He*
> *created for you mates from among yourselves,*
> *that ye may dwell in tranquility with them, and*
> *He has put love and mercy between your*
> *(hearts): Verily in that are signs for those who*
> *reflect. (Al Rum, 21)*
>
> *And Allah has made for you mates (and*
> *companions) of your own nature, and made*
> *for you, out of them sons and daughters and*
> *grandchildren, and provided for your*
> *sustenance of the best….(Al Nahl, 72)*
>
> *O ye who believe! Save yourselves and*
> *your families from a fire whose fuel is men*
> *and stones….(Al Tahrim, 6)*

It is important to note that the one, who officiates at the wedding, should mention one or two *Ahadith* of the Prophet before supplication. Also, the one who officiates at the wedding can give a speech (either before the sermon or at the end) that deals with both the husband's and wife's rights and obligations and that draws both of their attentions towards their shared responsibilities.

Obedience:

Marriage in Islam is based upon mutual respect. The Qur'an unmistakably advocates mutual respect between men and women. Marriage is an equal association, not one of a man's superiority over a woman. In Islam, no man has superiority over a woman, and no woman has superiority over a man except by piety, righteousness, and knowledge. Within the Muslim community many misunderstand the relationship between husbands and wives. Since people are taught that women must be obedient unconditionally, they are convinced of its correctness. There is no such thing as unconditional obedience in Islam. First of all, obedience is only to Allah. A woman is obedient to her husband as long as he is obedient to God. In matters relating to revelation, both are equally responsible. For anything outside Qur'nic revelation and the *sunnah* of the Prophet, there is the matter of consultation and communication that both need to follow. The Prophet used to consult not only with his wives but also with other women on social issues. Consultation is a decree from God in all matters of family or outside of family. The purpose of family is to have progress, happiness and welfare. Women are not slaves, maids, or personal servants of men. They have a role to fulfill at home. If their husbands are not home, wives are automatically the head of the household. A Muslim woman who lives according to Islamic life knows where to go, when to go and whom to meet. Thus, by obeying Islamic rules, the wife will not harm herself or jeopardize her family's social status. If a man acts improperly at home or violates any Islamic principle, the woman must not be obedient; on the contrary, politely and decisively, she must give him Islamic advice and remind her husband of his mistakes. By the same token, if the wife does something wrong, the husband must to counsel her. If she persists, he must separate her from his bed. Finally, according to the Qur'an, he must tap her gently (or completely separate from her) to draw her attention to their shared responsibilities.

Misunderstanding of the verse 4 of Al Nisa:

Neither God nor His Prophet is abusive. As a matter of fact, God in Islam is All Just and Absolute Just. If God is All Just and Absolute Just, can He be unjust and abusive at the same time? Obviously, the answer is no. Before the advent of Islam, His message was transmitted to a Prophet, previously called *Al Amin,* which means trustworthy. A Just Being gave His message to a highly trusted person such as Prophet Mohammad. A trustworthy person is neither abusive nor unjust. The foundation of Islam is knowledge. Pure knowledge cannot be biased, abusive or discriminatory. Finally, after the migration, Yathrib was renamed Medina. This simply means that Islam designs a civilized world and requires its adherents to act civilly. In a civilized world abuse, biases, and discrimination do not have any place. Therefore, it is beyond imagination and understanding that the Qur'an will ask men to "beat lightly" women if they are disobedient. Translation of verse 4 of Al Nisa follows. In the Qur'an Allah says:

As to those women on whose part you fear disloyalty and ill conduct, admonish them (first), (next), refuse to share their beds, (and last) beat them lightly; but if they return to obedience, seek not against them means (of annoyance): For Allah is Most High, Great (above you all). (Qur'an, 4:34)

Studying this verse, *nushuzahun* (disloyalty and ill-conduct) is addressed before *adhrebuhuna* (lightly beating). Disloyalty and ill conduct refer only to *tawhid* and its principle. According to Islam, men and women are obliged to obey Allah in order to have a harmonious life. A woman is in the stage of *nushuz* if, for example, she ignores praying without a permissible reason or violates any laws of Islam and becomes indifferent to Islam. Obedience does not mean that she should do exactly as her husband commands. The obedience of a wife is applicable only as long as all aspects of the husband's and the wife's lives are according to the law of God. *Nushzahun* also applies to men.[67] As mentioned earlier, if a husband violates the principle of *tawhid,* he is also in a state of *nushuz* and he is called *nashez* according to Islamic jurisprudence. In this case, the husband needs to be reminded of Islam. If he does not correct his behavior, the woman can seek a divorce.

The second issue of this verse that has been translated as "lightly beating" has been misunderstood. *Adhrabuhun* in this context does not mean beating

---

[67] Bahiri, Mohammad abdul Wahab. *Hila hai-e- shara nasazgar ba falsafe fiq* (Lawful deceit incompatible to the philosophy of Islamic jurisprudence). Trns into Persian by Hussain Saaberi. The Islamic Research Foundation, Mashhad, 1367 Islamic solar calendar.

lightly; it means tapping[68], or a complete separation according to others. When water is not available, Muslims take ablution with clean dust, and they lightly tap on dust and rub it on their faces. It is the same tapping that is in the context of verse 4. The purpose of tapping is to draw the wife's attention as a Muslim. Prophet Mohammad said, "Do not beat your wives as you would your servant girls in pre-Islamic times."[69] In this saying of the Prophet, there are two issues. One asks his followers not to beat their wives. The second tells them not to treat their wives as slave girls. Socio-psychologically it is important that a wife not be treated as a purchased good, that should do anything the master commands. Concerning the tapping, Imam Shafii, one of the most prominent scholars of the four schools of thought in Islam, considers tapping "inadvisable." (Translation and Commentary: Abdullah Yusuf Ali).

Mutual Relations in Intercourse:

Men and women are created from the same soul according to the Qur'an. They complement each other as spouses of each other. Allah asks men in chapter 4, Verse 49, to live with women in equity. The Almighty God refers to mutual relations of men and women,

---

[68] Yusuf, Hamza. Peaceful Families Conference, Islamic Society of East Bay (ISEB), Fremont, California, May 4-6, 2001.
[69] Jones & Philips. Plural Marriage in Islam. International Islamic Publishing House, Riyadh, PP.14, 1985.

saying, "You demand your mutual right" (4:1), and also, "And women shall have rights similar to the right against them, according to what is equitable" (2:228). Men have misunderstood their sexual relations and think they have the sole proprietorship of intercourse. This notion has arisen because of a misunderstanding of a *hadith* that the Prophet said, "If a woman refuses her husband bed and passes the night in anger, the angels curse her until morning."[70] Taken literally, this *hadith* means that men and women do not have any mutual understanding according to the above verses. It means that regardless of what happens to the woman, she has to make herself available to her husband; otherwise, the angels will curse her. The above *hadith* is contradictory to the Qur'an, which has established mutual respect between the sexes. Also, consider what should happen if the husband does not make himself available to his wife? What should she do? Does God curse the husband?

Women are garments for men, and men are garments for women. As such, husbands and wives have total mutual relations in bed. They need to enjoy each other, not force themselves on the other. The above hadith has three conditions. First, a woman should be free of menses. Second, a woman should be well. Third, she needs to be mentally ready for intercourse. A woman is not an animal; she doesn't have to make herself available whenever her husband desires her. The third condition is very important. Suppose that a woman loses her child or a parent. Is she mentally ready to have sex the same night? If

---

[70] Al-Bukhari, Sahih

67

anyone answers this question affirmatively, it seems that he/she does not understand the justice of Islam. Islam came to this world bringing justice for all and establishing mutual respect between couples and people in society. Islam wants people to live in peace and to enjoy the bounty of this life. Islam does not approve of abuse, disrespect, and mental torture as committed by the Taliban in Afghanistan under the name of Islam. Allah says:

> *"And among His signs is this, that He created for you mates from among yourselves, that you may dwell in tranquility with them, an He has put love and mercy between your (hearts): Verily in that are signs for those who reflect". (Qur'an, 30:21)*

Without a doubt, verse 30:21 emphasizes God's love and affection for both sexes. Human sexuality is not a one-way phenomenon where one person enjoys it while the other is deprived or forced to commit the act against his/her will. In California forcing a wife to go to bed is illegal; it is called marital rape. It is also important to mention that there are women who try to manipulate their husbands by not sharing the bed with them. No woman has the right to manipulate her husband. In keeping with the Qur'an, men and women should enjoy mutual relations. Men have rights over their wives just as a woman has rights over her husband. If a woman is displeased with her husband, she better communicate rather than deprive him of his right. Not sharing a bed with a husband without proper justification will cause the husband to doubt, and the relationship will become sour. Consultation, communication, and trust are the key components of any marriage.

Permission or Consultation:

It is universally accepted by the Muslim community that women should have permission of their husbands to do something, to go somewhere, and so on. Muslim men and women, who know Islam, know their rights and obligations. We do not live in a time of *jahillia* (ignorance). Both sexes have equal responsibilities. Even if a wife does not work outside her home, she is not a purchased good. She shouldn't be denied the right to make decisions or be forbidden from going where she needs to go. In this day and age, husbands and wives should consult each other on all matters, an Islamic concept. According to Islamic law, there are two restrictions. A Muslim woman cannot invite a strange man into their home without her husband's consent. Also, she cannot do a non-obligatory fasting if she has more important things to attend to such as educating her child.

Young Muslim girls criticize Islam because these types of restrictions make them feel exploited if they commit to marriage. Prophet Mohammad allowed women to go to the mosques in the evening. And remember, mosques are not only a place of worship but of education as well. Women were allowed to go shopping, visit their relatives, and do whatever they need to do for their family as long as they keep their modesty and do not jeopardize their family life. A wife's duty is to fulfill her husband's dream and wishes, just as it is a husband's duty to fulfill his obligations to his wife. Both should strive for the compete happiness of each other. There are women who say they love their husbands, but try to dominate him entirely. Sometimes these wives dominate their husbands to the extent that they cannot fulfill even their Islamic duty. This situation is not acceptable for a Muslim husband as it is contrary to Islamic law. Both husband and wife should try to fulfill each other's desires. Neither should dominate the other.

Marriage to non-Muslims: Gender Biased?

Frequently, secular minded Muslims and non-Muslims criticize Islam for its ruling that Muslim men can marry a Christian or a Jew while a Muslim woman cannot marry a non-Muslim.

This issue should be studied within a religious context in order to address this criticism comprehensively. What many non-Muslims fail to understand and cannot comprehend is that Islam is not only the continuation of other monotheistic religions, namely Judaism and Christianity, but also Islam is a religion in tune with the laws of nature and the nature of man. If one accepts that Islam is a continuation of past religions, then surely he/she will understand there is wisdom behind such rulings. God Almighty has a purpose for everything, and He knows what is best for His creation. The evolution of religion through which the Prophets went was completed with a message in the Qur'an when Allah said,

"This day have I perfected your religion for you, completed my favor upon you, and have chosen for you Islam as your religion" (Qur'an 5:3)

When God Almighty speaks of perfection of His religion for humanity, it would be ludicrous to question His wisdom. Those who acknowledge that Islam is a continuation of past revelations given all the way from Adam down to Mohammad will also acknowledge the universality of Islam. It is noteworthy to mention that Islam, in spite of these criticisms, is the fastest growing religion in the world, particularly in the United States, where a large number of converts are women. This fact reveals that if there were a contradiction or biased attitude within the religion against women, then these people would not be attracted to Islam.

The foundation of all societies is the family. As such, the foundation of a solid Islamic life starts with the family, which is the focal point of spiritual and intellectual growth. Marriage is a process of exogamy. When a woman leaves her household and enters her husband's household, she must adapt to all of the customs and principles of her new home. This is true for Muslims and non-Muslims alike. In Christianity, women adopt their husband's last name upon marriage; in Islam, women have the right to safeguard their individual rights by keeping their last name. Without any offense intended, it is evident that by understanding the path of religion and of God throughout history, it can be concluded that Islam is the most complete way of life for humanity. Therefore, if a Muslim woman enters into a non-Muslim household, this simply means she is leaving her complete way of life for something that is less than complete. Islam, however, is a religion of progression, not regression. By the same token, a Muslim man is allowed to marry a lady from the People of the Book, Christians and Jews, because she enters a more complete household. That is why Islamic religious scholars have unanimously agreed upon the fact that it is *haram* (forbidden) for a Muslim woman to marry outside her religion. Conversely, a Muslim man can marry a Jew or a Christian.

It is universally accepted that the head of the household is the man. Christianity, for example, requires a woman to obey her husband. The New Testament of the Bible in the *Epistle of Paul the Apostle to the Ephesians* states, "Wives, submit yourselves unto your own husbands, as unto the Lord. For the husband is the head of the wife, even as Christ is the head of the church: and he is the savior of the body. Therefore as the Church is subject unto Christ, so *let* the wives *be* to their own husbands in everything"(5:22-24). Islam does not require a woman to obey her husband unconditionally. She is required to obey her husband according to the laws of marriage in Islam and submit only to Allah. Islam recognizes both genders as equal. Referring to husbands and wives, the Qur'an states,

"They are your garments and you are their garments" (Qur'an2: 187)

This verse clearly indicates the equality of husband and wife in their mutual relationship. In this regard, God Almighty addresses both sexes saying,

"Fear Allah, through whom ye demand your mutual rights" (Qur'an 4:1)

It is therefore unadvisable to have a Muslim woman marrying a non-Muslim man, as she should not enter a household where she will be unconditionally subjected to the will of her husband. Instead, she should be an equal partner with equal rights.

As much as a Muslim reveres and respects other Prophets of God, it is unfortunate that the People of the Book altogether fail to acknowledge the final Messenger of God. The following verses from the Qur'an describe the attitude of the People of the Book:

"Quite a number of the People of the Book wish they could turn you (people) back to infidelity after you have believed...Never will the Jews or the Christians be satisfied with thee unless thou follow their form of religion...Even if thou were to bring to the people of the book all the signs (together), they would not follow thy Qiblah...the People of the Book know this [the truth] as they know their own sons; but some of them conceal the truth which they themselves know" (Qur'an2: 109,120,145,146)

Dr. Farid Younos

Also, the Qur'an says,

"Ye People of the Book! Why reject ye the Signs of Allah, of which ye are (yourselves) witnesses?" (Qur'an 3:70)

These verses should be sufficient to convince a Muslim woman who is a believer not to violate God's law and betray her religion while placing her family into a scandal. Finally, a Muslim woman is not only responsible for her own soul, family, and community, but she is also responsible for the children that she will bear. Therefore, it is her duty to raise a Muslim child in a Muslim atmosphere so that the child will recognize the evolution of religion throughout history and will acknowledge that Islam is the final message of God. In this way, both mother and child can live under Islam's complete way of life, where God's law and natural law are recognized as one and the same.

Who is a Minor? Islamic Vs. Western Culture:

The Islamic culture that is based upon the tradition of the Prophet Mohammad allows young girls at the age of puberty to marry. As a matter of fact, the Prophet married the daughter of Aisha of his best friend Abu Bakr, when she was thirteen years of age.

The American culture has established the legal age of marriage as eighteen. Obviously, in American culture, those below the age of eighteen are considered minors, and as such, cannot legally marry. Americans consider those who are thirteen to seventeen as minors and define them as teenagers. In modern American society, the legal and social systems establish the adult rather than letting the process of nature do so; hence, there is no clear-cut age border to cross. Americans have different ages for different social norms, i.e. marrying at eighteen, driving at sixteen, drinking at twenty-one, and so forth. There is no consistency and not much logical justification as to why these numbers were determined except by majority consent of empowered individuals.

The Islamic world does not look upon marriage as a quantitative, but rather a qualitative phenomenon that is based upon human development. Adolescence changes the body's chemistry. According to psychologists, this change of chemistry has a definite effect on human behavior and mentality. Therefore, it is important to note that physical changes in adolescence could be a turning point for many individuals. It is an age when either an individual goes toward intimacy or isolation (Erickson, 1968). When a young girl identifies herself as a mature person, her behavior and outlook will change. Psychological studies reveal that visible evidence of puberty appears between the ages of eight to thirteen with the development of breast buds. The next stage of maturation is with respect to height, which takes place about eighteen months later. This means that by age of fifteen or sixteen, a young girl will reach ninety-eight percent of her height. Menstruation also begins between the ages of ten and seventeen and depends upon the environment of growth and nourishment, which plays a role in human development (Morris,

1976). All these facts inform us that a young girl at the age of fourteen might have the same desires as an adult.

Because American culture allows irresponsible dating among their teenagers, many problems for the individual and for the family have arisen, while at the same time placing an enormous cost and burden on the social and legal systems. According to Reuters *Health*, "4 out of 10 Americans females will be pregnant before the age of 20. Close to 80% of teen mothers will require welfare assistance. The U.S. teen pregnancy rate remains the highest in the industrialized world,"(May 13, 2000). Teenage pregnancy has caused abortion and infant abandonment. American society considers pregnant teenagers as "outsiders" and some teen girls have tried to commit suicide because of social shame and disgust.

On the other hand, Islam forbids dating in the Western style; it does not legally deprive the individual from her/his sexual demands if they act responsibly. "Muslims of early centuries believed that sexual deprivation could lead to mental and physical disturbances, bordering on insanity. One observer related that a group of people had decided to abstain for ascetic reasons, but soon they developed physical as well as mental abnormalities, especially depression and fatigue" (Ati: 1977, P.51). The "legal age" according to Islam is determined by the maturity of an individual's physical development, which is normally reached between the ages of thirteen and fourteen for girls and fifteen to sixteen for boys. Society recognizes them as individuals, and not as teenagers. The Islamic educational system recommends a young boy or girl should start performing prayers at the age of seven, and his/her bed should be separated from his/her parents at the same age. By the age of thirteen or fourteen, both sexes should be aware of the basic Islamic principles such as prayer, fasting, menstruation, family manners, social manners and conduct, which include how to behave in school as well as in society.

Two more criticisms should be addressed at this point. First, some consider young couples unfit for married life. To answer for this concern it is imperative to examine the family structure of the Islamic world. Unlike the nuclear-family system that is common in the West, the Islamic world emphasizes the extended-family system—this means that the whole family shares the responsibilities of a young couple. For example, the whole family will help a young man at the age of sixteen if he is not ready to take care of his wife economically, as long as they are emotionally and physically mature enough to marry. Therefore, neither the young man nor the young girl will be deprived of their natural rights to join in matrimony and enjoy themselves. Also, some ask how the couple could love each other if they do not date. True love will develop through time. There are many couples in the West that have dated for many years, lived together without marriage for a couple of years, and then married. Oftentimes they divorce. Dating, therefore, is not a guarantee for a harmonious marriage.

The second concern deals with the concept that some consider older men marrying younger girls as unfair and abusive. Human sexuality does not recognize borders or age and it is not limited to time and space. There are many older men in the West, especially in Hollywood who are role models and icons; they have married younger girls or have several girlfriends or mistresses who are even forty years younger than they. The story of a female teacher in Washington State in love with a "teenage boy" is another case in point. Ironically, the judicial system punished her on the grounds of associating with a "minor." Despite many psychological studies, no one could defend her according to the laws of nature: her nature is correct in liking a younger man, just as an older man can like a younger girl. There are girls who like older men and have a "crush" on them. The term, "middle age crisis," has been used for those men and women who fall in love in their forties, fifties, or sixties, usually with someone much younger than themselves. Therefore, there is no such thing as the right age for human sexuality.

In Islam, marriage is allowed as long as it is with the consent of both parties. To protect the right of younger girls or women in general, the Prophet of Islam said, "No one can marry a virgin girl, a widow or a divorced woman without her consent." Therefore, if a girl agrees, that is her freedom of choice and she bears the responsibility. It is her legal and natural choice to become a mother. Before going further, it is important to note here that despite the fact that religious freedom is a vital component of the American system as well as a constitutional right, Muslims in the United States are not allowed to marry before the age of eighteen or to practice polygamy. Policy makers want Muslims to change their faith; they do not understand that for Muslims, religion is not merely a belief but a way of life. Also, they do not understand that the law of God and the law of nature are one and the same in Islam.

Inheritance:

Some criticize Islam because females receive less inheritance than males. To understand this concept, it is important to understand that inheritance laws in Western society were implemented much less than 100 years ago. Thus, in English law or French law, the basis of all Western laws in the contemporary world, women did not have any right of inheritance. In Islam, women were given inheritance rights 1,400 years ago—these were not discriminatory, but rather part of the formation of a fair and just foundation of society, the family. It is true that on the surface, women do receive less than men, but in reality women receive more than men.

When a girl marries, she is entitled to dowry as well as other gifts, which are usually in the form of jewelry. She has the right to ask for her dowry as a protection before the wedlock takes place. When she goes to her new family, she is entitled to her husband's inheritance. If she becomes widowed, she even has the right to inherent from her children. Therefore, in the long run, a woman inherits from four sources: dowry, the father, the husband, and in some cases, her children.

In the Islamic family structure, men not women are responsible for providing for the household. Therefore, a woman does not have any responsibility to carry the economic burden of her family and consequently the children, be they male or female must take care of their parents. Indirectly, this system is another source of inheritance if someone looks at these practices from an economic standpoint.

Islam tries to be fair and just. Nowadays, there are hundreds of women and men in Western societies who are lonely, and hundreds more who are living on social welfare. Consequently, the responsibility of the family unit existing as a strong social foundation has been undermined.

If a Muslim girl does not want to marry, she remains the responsibility of her parents as long as she lives with them, and later she becomes a responsibility of the family as a whole. In these cases the overall idea is not the distribution of wealth but the development of a fair family system, where everyone lives in peace and equity, not in isolation, poverty, or homelessness.

Of course, it must be remembered that the Islamic system will never work if any tenant of the Islamic principles is broken or mixed up with non-Islamic ideas. Islam as a complete way of life is functional if it is applied Islamically. Societies fail when, instead of finding their answers to problems in Islam, they try to borrow alien ideas that contradict the principles of the Islamic economic system or family life.

Polygamy:

Many Muslims and non-Muslims criticize polygamy as unfair mutual relations between couples in a social system. But as a matter of fact, polygamy, if it is applied correctly, solves many problems and keeps the family intact.

For this discussion it is better use the word *polygyny* rather than *polygamy* because Muslim men are allowed to marry up to four wives (but may very well marry just one) while Muslim women are allowed only one husband at a time. This issue of *polygyny* is allowed, not for lust or desire, but for solving family and social problems. A verse in the Qur'an clearly speaks about dealing with the issue justly. *Polygyny* is not a must or a social norm, but rather a solution to safeguard the principles of ethics and moral values.

Here is how *polygyny* works. No man can marry another woman without the consent of the first wife. Women are even allowed to put monogamy as a condition in their marriage contract if they do not want to associate with a polygamous man. For example, in the wedding ceremony a woman can put as a condition that she will not live with her husband if he marries a second wife.[71] Therefore, it is a woman's choice that with her consent and with due justification a second marriage can take place. Or she can file for divorce if she is not happy, even if she had not stipulated monogamy in her marriage contract.

There are many reasons that a second marriage becomes a necessary composition of a family life. The most common one given by scholars is in war. Many women become widowed and rather than being alone or resorting to prostitution, they need a husband. As

---

[71] Hassan, Hassan Ibrahim. Political History of Islam, Translated into Persian by Kasim Payinda, 1376 of Islamic solar calendar, Tehran.

well, there are familial reasons, such as not being able to bear a child. The point of this discussion is that a man can marry a second wife if he treats her as equally as the first. Otherwise, it is illegal morally to have a second wife because the husband cannot fulfill justice. The recent dilemma of widows and orphans in twenty-three years of war in Afghanistan is a case in point. Widows need not only material protection, but they also need a personal, intimate relationship. Islam has solved this problem by allowing a second marriage with the consent of the first wife. Also, sometimes a woman may not be able to fulfill her obligations as a wife, but she wants to keep her marriage without losing any benefits. Therefore, she allows her husband to have a second wife. Islam is a monotheistic religion with a patriarchal society and always favors the usual norms of nature. Therefore, Islam frowns on polyandry since it would cause chaos. To those who want to argue why women cannot marry a second husband, the answer is polyandry is against human nature and it would cause a great deal of legal hardships on the family as a whole (such as determining who the father is of a child).

Women Can Seek Divorce:

Divorce in Islam is widely misunderstood by Muslim men as well as by non-Muslims. Many think that women in Islam cannot ask for divorce unless their husbands initiate and/or agree to it. A case in point occurred when an Afghan woman in America received a divorce decree from a court of law in the United

States. The husband yelled at her, "You are still my wife according to Islam! I will never divorce you!" Ironically, in Islamic countries the majority rights are given to men since most people don't pay much attention to a woman's demands. Consequently, the divorce law is completely distorted. Men think that divorce in Islam is a husband's right, not the wife's.

Some background is necessary to understand divorce in Islam. First, marriage in Islam is a distinguished social contract. As long as both parties fulfill their duties to each other, there is no room for divorce. Sometimes there are personality clashes, and the husband and wife cannot live in harmony. In this instance both husband and wife must try to work out their differences before they resort to divorce. Even though Allah permits divorce, according to the Hadith of the Prophet Mohammad, divorce is one of those permissible issues that Allah hates the most. Hence, divorce should be the last resort to conflict resolution between couples.

If a woman presents her strong reasons for seeking a divorce, her husband must rectify the situation. If the wife still insists on a divorce, the husband has no legal right to deny the wife's right for a divorce. If the husband insists on keeping his wife, a judge must step in and accept the divorce request. Allah says in the Qur'an:

And if you (the judges) do indeed fear that the two may not be able to keep to the limits ordained by Allah, there is no blame on either of them if she redeems herself (from marriage contract by returning what she has received at the time of marriage.)(Qur'an 2:229)

The story of Thabit ibn Qias, a disciple of the Prophet, is well known among Muslim scholars and historians. Thabit ibn Qais's wife was not happy with her husband even though he was a very good man. She went to the Prophet Mohammad and presented her case, saying " 'O Allah's Apostle! I do not blame Thabit for defects in his character or his religion, but I being a Muslim, dislike to behave in an un-Islamic manner (if I remain with him).'" After hearing her complaint, the Prophet asked her if she had taken anything from Thabit. She replied affirmatively, mentioning the garden. The Prophet inquired if she were able to return that garden. Again, she replied affirmatively. Then the Prophet called upon Thabit and asked him to take his garden and divorce her. (Please see the Book of Divorce, Sahih Bukhari, vol. 7. p. 150).

Under Islamic law, when a woman asks for a divorce, it is called *Al-khul*. Verse 2:229 and the above Hadith show that there is total equality between husband and wife. If one partner in a marriage is permitted to divorce and if the same opportunity is not given to the other partner, justice is not fulfilled. It must be remembered that Islam is a way of life that encompasses justice for all.

Guest in the Family:

Many Muslims when receiving guests do not allow their wives to come and welcome their male guests. This is noticeable even among those Muslims who completed their education in Islamic Studies!

The wife playing an important role in both hospitality and in receiving guests is clearly advised in the Qur'an in the story of Prophet Abraham where angels approached him and gave him the news of a son. The Qur'an states in verse 24 through 30 of the chapter *Al-dharyiat* (The Winds that Scatter) that:

"Has the story reached thee, of the honoured guests of Abraham?"

"Behold, They entered His presence, and said: 'peace!' He said 'Peace!' (And though, they seem) unusual people."

"Then he turned quickly to his household, [wife] brought out a fatted calf,"

"And placed it before them…. He said, 'Will ye not eat'"

"(when they did not eat), He conceived a fear of them. They said, 'fear not,' and they give him glad tidings of a son endowed with knowledge."

"But his wife came forward (laughing) aloud: she mote her forehead and said; 'A barren old woman'"

"They said, 'even so has thy Lord spoken: and He is full of wisdom and knowledge'"

It is not forbidden for Muslim couples to receive their male and female guests and welcome them to their home in the presence of each other. This ruling is based upon the wedding of Usayd al-Sa'adi to which the Prophet of Islam and some of his companions were invited and in which his wife served them meals. (Please see the lawful and the prohibited in Islam by Dr. Yusuf Al-Qardawi, American Trust publications. Indiana 1994, p. 168).

As long as a woman and a man are properly dressed and they keep their discussion within modest limits, there is no restriction for them to associate with each other. Neither husband nor wife is allowed to receive a person of the opposite sex at home while alone. It is also *haram* (forbidden) for men to come to their guests wearing shorts or any other improper dress. Conversation should be in good nature that promotes knowledge, learning and exchange of ideas not of lust and immoral issues such as backbiting and gossip. Also, the host serves permissible meals not prohibited food and drinks such as pork meat or alcoholic beverages. As stated earlier, only the Prophet's wives were secluded from public—this was not true of any other citizen of the Islamic community. Muslims should always associate with good moral people, not with those who have ill character and morality. The Qur'an says:

"The believers, men and women, are protectors of one another: they enjoy what is just, and forbid what is evil" (Qur'an 9:71)

Arranged Marriage:

An arranged marriage is simply matchmaking, a common practice all over the world. Matchmaking in Japan is a tradition. In the United States, matchmaking occurs when families and friends introduce couples to each other and even with profit-making companies that arrange introductions that will benefit the company. There is, however, a difference in matchmaking between Muslim and non-Muslim societies. In non-Muslim societies, people date without any commitment. In Islamic societies when families match a couple, the purpose is marriage, not dating. Each party gives the other relevant information. Also, the couple must see each other before agreeing to the marriage because it is a tradition of the Prophet that a man should see the woman whom he will marry. As well, according to Islamic law, no one can marry a virgin girl, a widow, or a divorced woman without her permission. Therefore, an arranged marriage is a means to facilitate a relationship between a couple and serves as a safe and secure screening process for both parties. An arranged marriage does not mean that the man and the woman marry each other without each of them giving consent. Before marriage and before making a commitment, a couple is allowed to sit in the presence of others and exchange their views. Parents have misunderstood the phenomenon of the arranged marriage and have violated Islamic law by marrying their daughter to whomever they pleased regardless of their daughter's wishes. Misapplication of the arranged marriage occurs not only in Islamic countries but also in countries such as India and China.

According to Muslims, Islam is universal because it was revealed to mankind, not to a tribe, not to a specific region, and not to a specific people. Islam came to civilize people by eliminating illiteracy and ignorance as well as tribal attitudes. Unfortunately, nowadays people in the Islamic world do not practice fully Islamic behavior; rather, they keep their tribal and regional attitudes. After fourteen hundred years, Islam and regional cultures are mixed; this mixture has placed indigenous culture over Islamic culture, resulting in many problems and a bad name for Islam. Islamic culture, if implemented Islamically, is intended to give a community dignity, respect, and harmony so that all can live in peace and felicity and justice.

CONCLUSION

Islam came to this world not only to complete God's message to humanity after the revelations to Moses and Jesus, but also to redeem mankind from any sort of servitude, slavery, and exploitation. The message of Islam is crystal clear: Submission and worship are due only to God Almighty who is the Creator, the Provider, the Sustainer, the Protector, and the Law Giver. The law of nature and the law of God are one and the same. He is the One who created the entire universe, mankind included. God knows what is best for His creation; therefore, all laws that have been ordained for humanity are designed for human needs, progress, felicity, and spiritual growth.

God is just and has mercy and compassion over His creation. A Just God does not discriminate over His own creation; otherwise, He would not be called a Just God. All His messengers, from Adam to Abraham, Moses to Jesus, and Mohammad, had one clear message: To worship Him alone. If they rejected the message revealed by God, the consequences would mean misery, servitude, exploitation, and humiliation. Worshipping only God means to obey His Law and to submit to His Law in all walks of life. Submission to God means to obey, to learn, to explore, to carry His message, and to fulfill His mission on earth as His vicegerent. God's mission on earth is peace and justice. He made mankind to fulfill His mission, which brings peace and justice to the world. The literal meaning of Islam is peace; the allegorical meaning of Islam is Submission to the Will of God. Mankind can be at peace only if he/she submits to his/her Creator, Who is the source of peace, and only if he/she accepts that His laws and the laws of nature are one and the same.

God created mankind, to worship Him. He created two genders to complement each other and to complete each other as equal partners for fulfilling His mission on earth. Marriage corresponds to the law of nature and serves the purpose of God's laws of creation. For this purpose, He created men and women from a single soul without any discrimination, duality, or prejudice.

According to Islam, the foundation of a civilized society is the family, the smallest unit of society. Through the family, mankind achieves felicity. In an Islamic family, the man and the woman clothe each other with protection, support each other, and grow together. In addition, according to the law of God, when a couple unites, they offer their offspring as moral characters to establish an upright society.

Both genders are vicegerents of God on earth and have a social responsibility to each other. This responsibility and the couple's relationship should be based upon knowledge, modesty, and mutual respect for the rights of each other. Additionally, their relationship must be devoid of abuse, disrespect, and vengeful isolation. Through a couple's mutual acknowledgment of each other, Islam establishes social relations based upon ethical and moral virtues. The Prophet of Islam said that he came to this world to fulfill and complete the good deeds encompassing moral virtues. To accomplish the Prophet's mission, members of a society must recognize each other as family members. The Qur'an addresses the Muslim community saying that the members are sisters and brothers to each other. It is through a real sisterhood and brotherhood that Muslims reach felicity.

Islam is unlike any other civilization. For the last 300 years, however, Islam lost its supremacy as a world civilization because it no longer contributed to the infrastructure of the modern world. In addition, Islamic nations indulged in so many social malaises that the Islamic nations became the most backward in the world. Illiteracy, disease, economic dependency, war, famine, poverty, social injustices, gender discrimination, and prejudices against other schools of thought infect Muslims today. Muslim governments are off track, and Muslims are bereft of proper leadership. For example, some groups that came into existence as Islamic parties could not bring about constructive platforms for development; rather, all used militia strategy to come to power and forced people to follow their outline for Islam. All these groups are against women's participation in the social infrastructure of society.

The men of knowledge who could not and will not meet the demands of the contemporary world are to blame for the misery of the Islamic nations. Gender equality in the Islamic world is one issue that has been misconstrued. Clearly, on the basis of the Qur'an and the traditions of the Prophet, there should be no discrimination, prejudices, or biases against women. Regrettably, in practice the opposite is true.

Hopefully, the facts and ideas in this research will open many closed minds of Muslims and non-Muslims alike. Muslims need to leave their differences aside. They need to recognize and respect one another as individuals with equal rights within the family and within society. And non-Muslims, particularly the media, should not make hurried conclusions by biased reasoning or by attacking the laws of Islam calling them "barbarian laws" (San Francisco Chronicle, May 1, 2002). With this type of approach we cannot bring peace and harmony in our communities. The role of the media should be to reconcile people throughout the world through proper analysis and reporting.

Therefore, it is imperative that Muslims and non-Muslims make changes in their attitudes if justice for all people, all races, and both genders is to be achieved. As the Qur'an says:

"Allah will not change the fate of a people until they change what is in themselves." (Qur'an 13:11)

ABOUT THE AUTHOR

Dr. Farid Younos is a Muslim Afghan-American who fled his mother country shortly before the Soviet invasion of Afghanistan in 1979. He studied cultural anthropology in Denmark and obtained his doctorate degree in international and multicultural education from the University of San Francisco. He is a researcher and lecturer of Islamic studies and founder of Afghan Domestic Violence Prevention in the United States.

He serves as the president of Islamic research for the Afghan Journalist Foundation in the United States. An author, a TV host show, an advocate of women's rights and lecturer of Islamic thought; after the September 11th, Dr. Younos has responded by educating others about Islam and Afghanistan and become a prominent voice in the Bay Area of northern California. He has over sixty publications in Dari and English. His new *book Gender Equality in Islam* sets out to demonstrate that men and women are viewed and treated equals within the realm of Islamic law. He does this through an examination of men and women in creation, in family, and in society.

Printed in the United States
130579LV00001B/55/A

9 781403 357045